fASHION GeEK
clothing. accessories. tech.

fashion geek
clothing. accessories. tech.

DIANA ENG

North Light Books
Cincinnati, Ohio

www.mycraftivity.com

13 12 11 10 09   5 4 3 2 1

Distributed in Canada by Fraser Direct
100 Armstrong Avenue
Georgetown, ON, Canada L7G 5S4
Tel: (905) 877-4411

Distributed in the U.K. and Europe by David & Charles
Brunel House, Newton Abbot, Devon, TQ12 4PU, England
Tel: (+44) 1626 323200, Fax: (+44) 1626 323319
E-mail: postmaster@davidandcharles.co.uk

Distributed in Australia by Capricorn Link
P.O. Box 704, S. Windsor, NSW 2756 Australia
Tel: (02) 4577-3555

Library of Congress Cataloging-in-Publication Data
Eng, Diana.
　Fashion geek : clothes accessories tech / Diana Eng.
　　　p. cm.
　Includes index.
　ISBN 978-1-60061-083-7 (pbk. : alk. paper)
　1. Dress accessories--Technological innovations.
　2. Clothing and dress--Technological innovations.
　3. Sewing. 4. Light-emitting diodes--Amateurs'
manuals. 5. Electronics--Amateurs' manuals.
I. Title.
　TT560.E64 2009
　646.4'04--dc22
　　　　　　　　　　　　　　2008042819

Editors: Robin M. Hampton, Christine Doyle
Designer: Karla Baker
Layout Artist: Geoff Raker
Production Coordinator: Greg Nock
Photography Art Direction: Marissa Bowers
Photographer: Ric Deliantoni, Tim Grondin
Wardrobe Stylist: Monica Skrezlowski
Hair and Makeup: Lynn Molitor, Nikki Deitsch

METRIC CONVERSION CHART

to convert	to	multiply by
Inches	Centimeters	2.54
Centimeters	Inches	0.4
Feet	Centimeters	30.5
Centimeters	Feet	0.03
Yards	Meters	0.9
Meters	Yards	1.1
Sq. Inches	Sq. Centimeters	6.45
Sq. Centimeters	Sq. Inches	0.16
Sq. Feet	Sq. Meters	0.09
Sq. Meters	Sq. Feet	10.8
Sq. Yards	Sq. Meters	0.8
Sq. Meters	Sq. Yards	1.2
Pounds	Kilograms	0.45
Kilograms	Pounds	2.2
Ounces	Grams	28.6
Grams	Ounces	0.035

fw
media
www.fwmedia.com

about the author

Diana Eng is a fashion designer who specializes in technology, math and science. Her designs range from inflatable clothing to fashions inspired by the mechanical engineering of biomimetics. At age 22, her inflatable dress made the cover of *ID Magazine*. In 2005, she appeared as a designer contestant on season two of the Emmy-nominated hit TV show, *Project Runway*. She won Yahoo Hack Day in 2006, along with her two teammates, for designing and creating a blogging purse in less than 24 hours. Her work has been featured in exhibits both in the U.S. and internationally and has graced the pages of such publications as *Women's Wear Daily*, *Wired*, and *Craft:* magazine. She is the author of *TechStyle: Create Wired Wearables and Geeky Gear*. Diana is currently a designer in research and development in the New York City fashion industry and a founding member of Brooklyn-based hacker group NYC Resistor. To see more of Diana's work, visit: www.FashionNerd.com.

dedication

For those who want to make technology stylish.

acknowledgments

Thank you to my family for all of your support, to my grandmother for teaching me how to sew, and to my friends who were my first models trying on both the clothes that worked and my failed experiments. I would also like to thank my editors Robin Hampton and Christine Doyle for working so patiently with me. And thanks to North Light Books for making this such a fun project. Most of all, I would like to thank my mother, Dorian Eng, for all of her help getting things done and for being a mother.

accessories

CLOTHING

Miss Diana Eng is not your average everyday designer. She is an unusual combination of fashion and technology. Most designers like me are not computer savvy; we have a very rudimentary understanding of technology. With Miss Diana, I truly feel she is a techie at heart and then a fashion designer. What I love about Miss Diana's design is that it incorporates technology into a garment to enhance the wearer experience. I love her idea of installing a heart monitor and a camera in a hoodie. Whenever the wearer's heart rate increases, the camera takes a picture. Genius and modern because we live in a very interactive and voyeuristic world. Diana's designs are not just clothes; they act more like an interactive partner in one's life.

I met Miss Diana during *Project Runway*. She was one of my fellow contestants and my roommate. I must admit when I first met Miss Diana I thought she was kind of geeky, and I was dying to see her aesthetic as a designer. When I finally saw her first garment, the "Muslin Challenge," I was blown away by her creativity. She did something completely different than everyone else there. Her designs were very high art; conceptual but, for me, wonderfully wearable. What made it truly Diana's was her magnetic closures. Of course anyone who watches the show realized at that moment this was not a typical designer, especially when she started explaining why the magnets were not working.

People are always asking me why I chose Miss Diana as the designer to help with my "13th Challenge." What most people don't know about

Diana is that she is fast, creative and super crafty. My worktable was next to Diana's during the filming of the show, and I had firsthand experience of her abilities. On the "Barbie" challenge, Miss Diana had five minutes left before the runway, and within that small amount of time, she covered a clutch with silk charmeuse flawlessly with double-sided tape, French braided and teased her model's wig, and finished her Barbie doll-sized outfit that was an exact duplicate of that of her model. I still don't know how she did all that.

I always thought that *Project Runway* was an unfair platform for Miss Diana to truly showcase her talents of combining fashion and technology. Unfortunately for Diana, we were only allowed to go a fabric store for supplies; we were working with traditional material. That is why I am so happy for her to have this book to really show the world what she can do. I can't wait to sit down and do the projects and learn about all the things that I don't know. Diana has opened a whole new world for me when it comes to the endless possibilities of fashion and technology. She will do the same for you. Enjoy!

Diana, I am waiting for my hoodie.

CHLOE DAO

The combination of fashion and technology was until recently found only at high fashion runway shows and research labs. Now it's appearing in music videos and on the red carpet, and it's just starting to enter stores—and with this book, it's something that you can make. The projects in this book were inspired by runway fashion and accessories, and they use technology from our everyday lives and new electronic materials that have recently become more available to the general public.

I started playing with fashion and technology in college. While I was learning the basics of sewing, tailoring, draping and drafting patterns as an apparel design student at Rhode Island School of Design (RISD), I decided to try an electronics for artists class. In this class, I co-created an inflatable dress, and I began thinking about ways fashion and electronics could be combined.

I started doing some research to find out who else was making things with fashion and technology. I came across Thad Starner's wearable computers group at Georgia Tech; they were kind enough to let me visit them one afternoon when I was in Atlanta. Then I went to the International Symposium on Wearable Computers and met someone from the MIT media lab who was creating an emotion-sensing computer. The media lab was only forty-five minutes from RISD, and I was able to visit and offer thoughts on how to make the emotion-sensing wearable computer more wearer friendly. There I was introduced to Christine Liu and Nick Knouf, who asked me to participate in their MIT Seamless: Computational Couture fashion show. My newfound friends introduced me to all sorts of technology in fashion, from 3-D printing and laser cutting to conductive thread and fabric touch sensors. It completely changed how I thought about fashion.

But it wasn't until *Project Runway* that I really learned how to design and accessorize. Each week we created a garment for our model, styled her so that she had an outfit, and chose her hair and makeup. I really learned what worked and what did not, along with the importance of trends. Now I spend my days living and breathing fashion design in the fashion industry on Seventh Avenue in New York City. I go to shows during Fashion Week, fit clothes on models, shop for inspiration, choose trims, select fabric, sketch designs, and read magazines for the latest trends.

At night I hack electronics, taking apart things like cell phones, digital cameras and heartbeat monitors, and then I sew them into clothing. I do lots of experiments to see what sorts of things can be combined with fashion, and that's how I came across many of the designs for this book.

In this book are projects inspired by my experiences both in the fashion industry and in play with electronics. Included are an adaptation of the lightning bug dress that I wore to Heidi Klum's Halloween party, a headphone hoodie that uses the conductive thread I learned about at MIT, and twinkling shoes that use the pedometer sensor suggested by Emily Albinski on our Yahoo Hack Day team. What I hope these projects will be for you are the starting points to your own experimentations with fashion and technology. Have fun!

SEWING SUPPLIES AND TECHNIQUES

You will be sewing for a lot of the projects in this book, and once you learn how to sew, the clothing that you can create is limitless. You can sew by hand for small, detailed projects or sew by machine to get larger sewing projects done faster. A lot of tools and techniques are the same for hand sewing and machine sewing, and you will learn how to use them here. We will cover everything from using patterns and pinning fabric to threading a needle and starting and ending stitches so that they don't unravel. After reading this section, you will know what type of stitch to use for which type of fabric and the proper way to iron. Sewing is fun and easy. Here are the basics that you need to get started.

SEWING SUPPLIES

Pins
Straight sewing pins help hold everything in place. They come in a variety of thicknesses, but I like to use the thin ones because a machine can sew over them.

Fabric Scissors
These are long scissors, usually metal, that are specifically for cutting fabric. You should not cut paper with your fabric scissors because paper will dull them. Some brands that I like are Fiskars and Mundial.

Embroidery Scissors
These small scissors are good for cutting loose threads and other small things.

Seam Ripper
For fixing mistakes, a seam ripper is like the eraser of the sewing world. It literally rips out stitches you've made in the wrong place. It also can be used to take apart store-bought clothing.

Sewing Needle
Used for hand sewing, these needles come in a variety of sizes. A size 7 needle is the perfect size for sewing with conductive thread and for all the projects in this book.

Sewing Machine
You will use a sewing machine in some of the projects in this book. If you don't have a sewing machine already, be sure to choose one with a zigzag stitch and a backstitch.

Thread
Polyester thread is good to use, whether you're sewing by hand or machine, because cotton thread sometimes shrinks.

HAND SEWING

Hand stitching is a great skill to have for any kind of sewing you want to do. On these pages you will learn how to thread a needle, knot the thread, sew stitches, and knot off when you are done sewing. Once you've mastered these techniques, you'll find yourself using them over and over to sew small projects, details on larger projects, and much more.

THREADING A NEEDLE

Threading a needle can be difficult, especially with conductive thread, which unravels more easily than regular thread. Here are some tips to help you get the thread through the eye of a needle.

*Cut the end of the thread at an angle. This will make a small point at the end of the thread that will be easier to slide through the eye of the needle.

*To keep the end of the thread from unraveling, many people will lick the end. However, do not lick conductive thread, which is usually part metal. Instead, try licking your finger then touching the thread. You can twist the end of the thread between your pointer finger and your thumb to twist the fibers together if the thread becomes unraveled.

KNOTTING THREAD

Another finger-licking trick works here. Once you've threaded the needle, pull the two ends of the thread so that they meet. Lick the end of your pointer finger. Hold the ends of the thread at the first joint of your pointer finger, and wrap the thread around your pointer finger. Slide your thumb up and over the tip of your pointer finger, twisting the threads together between your thumb and finger. You will now have a twisted loop at the end of your thread. Pull down on the loop to make a knot. Now you're already to start sewing. If this doesn't work the first time, give it another try. It takes a bit of practice.

SEWING A RUNNING STITCH

A running stitch is used to sew two small pieces of fabric together and to create a circuit with conductive thread. Create a running stitch by inserting the needle under and over the fabric several times before pulling the thread through to create several stitches (about ⅛" [3mm] to ¼" [6mm] apart) at one time. Then pull the needle through the fabric to create the stitches.

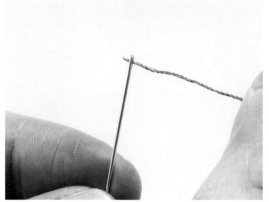
Threading a needle with conductive thread

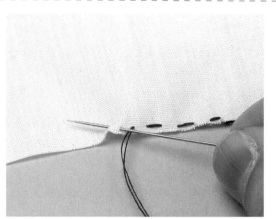
Sewing a running stitch

Sewing a whipstitch

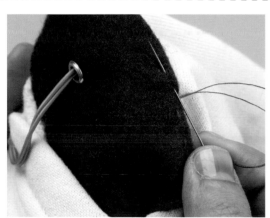
Sewing a topstitch

SEWING A WHIPSTITCH

This basic handsewing stitch helps to keep the ends of fabric from unraveling. To create this stitch, thread the needle and knot the thread. Push the needle through from the underside of the fabric (to hide the knot) to the top, near the edge of the fabric. Wrap the thread around the edge of the fabric and push the needle up from the underside again. Continue to push the needle from the underside until the edge of the fabric is wrapped in thread.

TOPSTITCHING

This stitch is used to sew one piece of fabric on top of another, like an appliqué. To create this stitch, thread the needle and knot the thread. Push the needle from the underside of the bottom fabric (to hide the knot) through the bottom fabric and the top fabric, near the edge of the top fabric. Use short running stitches to secure the fabrics together. When sewing a larger piece of fabric on top, use pins to hold the fabric in place while you sew.

KNOTTING OFF

When you reach the end of your stitches, create a secure knot that will keep the stitches from coming undone. To make this knot after your last stitch, slide your needle halfway through a small piece of fabric. Wrap the thread around the needle three or four times, and pull the needle through creating a knot.

BACKSTITCHING

Instead of knotting off, you can also backstitch to secure the stitches in place. Backstitch by stitching through your last stitch three or four times, then trim the thread close to the fabric.

MACHINE SEWING

Sewing by machine is much faster than sewing by hand. Machine sewing is kind of like driving: There is a foot pedal, and you steer the fabric left or right. All the basics are covered here, from starting and stopping to turning tight corners. You will learn about seam allowances and different stitches for different fabrics. Learning how to sew by machine doesn't take long, but you may want to practice on scrap fabric before you work on the good stuff.

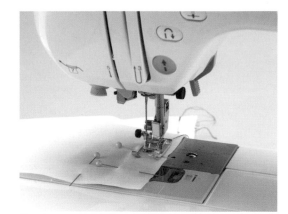

Sewing a seam allowance

SEWING A SEAM ALLOWANCE

Most sewing machines have, underneath the foot, a needle plate that has little lines on it. You can use any of the lines as a guide while sewing to help you keep your stitches the correct distance from the edge of the fabric; this distance is called the seam allowance. When sewing clothing, the seam allowance is usually ⅝" (2cm). It can be smaller for smaller projects like the petals of the *Light-Up Petal Purse* (see page 67). The lines on the needle plate usually have numbers on them to indicate how far the line is from the needle, so if you want to sew with a ⅝" (2cm) seam allowance, line up the edge of the fabric with the line marked "⅝"" (2cm). You will be stitching ⅝" (2cm) away from the edge of the fabric.

Marking the seam allowance

If you don't have any lines on your needle plate, measure the desired seam allowance distance from the point of the needle toward the machine and mark the plate with a piece of tape. Then use this tape as a guide while you are sewing.

BACKSTITCHING

Backstitching with a sewing machine gives the same result as knotting the thread when you are handsewing; it prevents the stitches from unraveling. By machine, you will start and finish sewing with a backstitch to prevent your stitches from coming undone. A sewing machine usually has a lever or knob that makes the machine sew in reverse. You can find information about this in the operating instructions for your sewing machine. When you start sewing, sew a few stitches forward, push the lever and backstitch a few stitches, then release the lever and continue sewing forward. When you are finished, push the lever and backstitch a few stitches, then cut the thread and you are done.

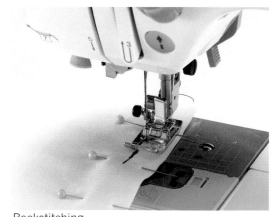

Backstitching

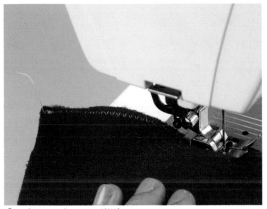

Sewing a zigzag stitch

ZIGZAG STITCHING

Most of the machine stitching you will do for these projects will be using a basic straight stitch. However, if you are stitching stretchy fabric, like the fleece for the *Monster Music Hat* on page 50, you should use a zigzag stitch. Straight stitches will break if stretched, but zig-zag stitching will stretch with the fabric. To create a zigzag stitch, consult your machine's operating instructions to find the proper setting, and make sure you are using a presser foot that can acco-modate a zigzag stitch. Then sew as usual; the needle will move side to side as well as up and down.

Sewing around a corner

SEWING CORNERS

If you are sewing along one side of the fabric, stitch until you reach the corner. Then lower the needle so that it is going through the fabric, lift the presser foot, and rotate the fabric so that the foot is lined up with the other side of the corner. Lower the presser foot, and continue sewing.

STITCHING AROUND TIGHT CURVES

Sewing along a tight curve can be difficult because it is not always easy to rotate the fabric while you are sewing. You can make rotating the fabric easier by lifting the presser foot of the sewing machine. To do so, stop the machine when the needle is down through the fabric. Lift the presser foot and rotate the fabric slightly by pivoting the fabric on the needle. Put the presser foot back down, and sew a few stitches. When the needle is down through the fabric again, lift the presser foot and rotate the fabric. Continue lifting, turning, and stitching until you have finished the curve.

Sewing isn't only about making nice stitches; it's also about knowing how to work with the fabric. There are many little tricks that can make a sewn piece go from fine to fantastic. On these pages you'll learn to pin the fabric pieces together for more accurate stitching and to press the seam allowances. You will also learn how to clip the seam allowances of curves so they will look nice when turned right side out.

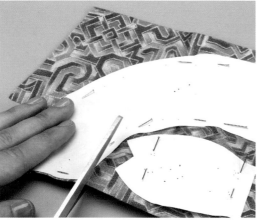

Pinning and cutting patterns

Pressing seam allowances

PINNING AND CUTTING PATTERNS

The first step to having accurate pattern pieces is to carefully cut out the paper patterns. Next, spread the fabric out on a hard, flat surface, such as a tabletop. Place all of your pattern pieces on the fabric, and try to conserve the fabric by placing pieces as close together as possible without overlapping them. Next pin the paper pattern pieces to the fabric to ensure that they stay in place while you cut. You will need to pin the pattern piece in many different places. To cut, hold the scissors perpendicular to the fabric, resting one side of the scissors flat on the tabletop. Place your other hand flat on the pattern piece to hold it in place.

If a pattern piece has an edge that is marked "fold," this edge should be lined up with the fold of the fabric.

PRESSING SEAM ALLOWANCES

Pressing seam allowances is what makes a garment look neat and well made. You might have the best design in the world, but if the seams are bunchy or the hems are uneven, that's the first thing people will notice. After you sew a seam, iron the seam allowances open—away from each other—before sewing that section to another pattern piece. This will keep seams nice, neat and professional looking.

PINNING FABRIC PIECES

When pinning two fabric pieces that you will stitch together, always insert the pin where you think the stitch line will be. This holds the fabric in place exactly where it will be sewn and is the most accurate way to pin. (It doesn't matter where you push the pin up and out.) If you are using a sewing machine and a running stitch, you can pin perpendicular to the stitch line and use very thin pins. Then you can sew right over the pins without removing them. This is not recommended, however, for a zigzag stitch.

TURNING CURVES AND CORNERS RIGHT SIDE OUT

If you have sewn tight curves, like those needed for the petals of the *Light-Up Petal Purse* (on page 60), you will need to make small snips in the seam allowance so that you will be able to turn curves the right side out and still have a nice curved shape. Before turning corners right side out, like for the tips of the petal, snip off the corner of the seam allowance just above the stitch line. This will get rid of extra fabric bulk.

USING A SEAM RIPPER

Everybody makes mistakes, and you may sew where you did not intend to. This is easy to undo with a seam ripper. Slide the point of the seam ripper under a stitch. Then continue sliding in an upward motion until you cut the stitch. Continue doing this until you've removed all the unwanted stitches.

Pinning fabric for machine stitching

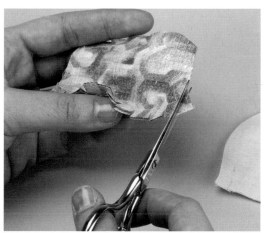

Cutting curves to prepare for turning right side out

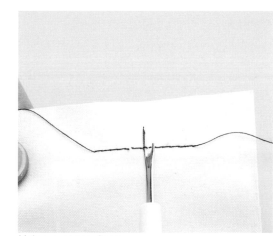

Using a seam ripper

ELECTRONIC SUPPLIES AND TECHNIQUES

Electricity is what makes lights turn on and computers work. It powers mobile phones and carries information across the Internet. We are going to use electricity in clothing, so it's important to learn just a little bit about how electricity works and how to work with it.

Electricity flows through wires, like water flows through pipes. You can connect wires together so that electricity can flow from one wire to the next, just like you can connect pipes. This section will teach you how to connect wires and electronic parts so that you can control the flow of electricity in your fashion designs. First, you'll learn about some of the supplies you'll need for the tech part of these projects, then you'll learn some basic techniques for using these supplies.

ELECTRONIC SUPPLIES

Alligator Clip Jumper Wires
These wires with clips on the ends help you test circuits. See page 29 for how to use them.

Battery
Use CR2032 coin cell batteries for all of the projects in this book. These batteries are small and compact but powerful enough for lighting up an LED. You can purchase these batteries anywhere you buy batteries, including drug stores, hardware stores and electronic stores.

Battery Holder
Use battery holder BS7. While there are many battery holders for a CR2032 battery, the BS7 battery holder is the easiest to sew. The holders can sometimes be found where you purchase the batteries, or you can get them from online electronic supply stores (see Resources, page 124).

Conductive Thread
This thread is unique in that it allows electricity to flow through it, like wire does. Conductive thread usually has metal bonded with it, incorporated into the fiber of the thread on the molecular level. You can purchase conductive thread from online stores (see Resources, page 124).

LED
Pronounced "el-ee-dee," and short for *light-emitting diode*, an LED is an electronic component that lights up. Electricity can flow through an LED in only one direction. Therefore, the positive side of the circuit must be connected to the long lead of an LED and the negative side of the circuit must be connected to the short lead.

EL Wire
EL wire, or electroluminescent wire, is copper wire covered in phosphor that glows with electricity. EL wire needs a driver to run. This is a small box that it plugs into that regulates the electricity and usually has a place to stick the batteries.

Wire
Electric wire has a conductive metal material on the inside to carry electric current and a nonconductive material on the outside called insulation. The insulation protects the electronic connection inside and protects you from getting an electric shock (if there is high voltage or current).

SOLDERING TOOLS

Solder
The "glue" for electronics, solder is used to connect electronic parts because it allows electricity to flow

through the connection. Solder is a solid metal, so to use it you will need to melt it with a soldering iron. There are different kinds of solder, so be sure to buy electrical solder instead of plumbing or jewelry solder. You can purchase electrical solder at electronic or hardware stores.

Soldering Iron
This tool melts solder, allowing you to form the solder and make the connections. Like an oven, most soldering irons need to be preheated; otherwise they will not be hot enough to melt the solder. When purchasing a soldering iron, make sure to get one that is 25 watts and has a small tip that will create the fine connections you'll need for these projects.

Wet Sponge
You can use a wet sponge to clean the tip of a soldering iron. If the tip of the iron starts to turn a different color (brown, black, anything other than its original color), it is time to give it a quick wipe on the sponge. Keep the sponge on your board (see below), and quickly wipe the iron's tip across the sponge. You can also wipe the iron on the sponge anytime you get too much solder on the iron.

Wooden Board
Always solder on top of a wooden board. The board will protect your work surface from getting

burned. Pressed cardboard (not corrugated) will work as well.

Eye Protection
Always wear goggles or glasses when soldering. While unlikely, a piece of hot solder could splatter and land in your eye.

Helping Hands
Helping hands is a stand with little clamps that helps you hold all of your components and parts when soldering. Not only does it create an extra pair of hands, but it helps keep you from getting burned by hot components.

OTHER TOOLS AND SUPPLIES

Electrical Tape
Use this insulating tape to wrap wires and connections to protect the conductive materials from damage.

Pliers
A tool used to help grip and hold small objects, regular pliers often have a built-in wire cutter, which is very handy and used in this book's projects to cut, bend and strip wires.

Needle-Nose Pliers
Needle-nose pliers or thin jewelry pliers are pliers with an extremely long and narrow gripping nose. You'll use them to bend the leads and wires.

Wire Cutter
A tool used specifically for cutting wire. You would not want to use scissors because the wire would ruin them.

Wire Stripper
Use wire strippers to remove the plastic coating or insulation from electric wires so that you can access the wire underneath for a better electronic connection.

Sandpaper
You will use this to create a matte finish on a few of the projects in this book. Please use extra fine sandpaper.

Rotary Tool
This handheld tool will be used to cut and sand a few of the projects in this book. The Dremel brand rotary tool is widely used. It comes with several different attachments for small scale cutting, sanding and drilling.

STRIPPING WIRE

Many wires come with a plastic coating, called insulation, that protects the electrical connection and protects you from getting shocked. To connect two wires, you will need to remove the insulation so that the metal part inside one wire can touch the metal part inside the other wire. You can easily strip wire with wire strippers, a tool created just for this task, as shown below. With more practice you can also just use wire cutters.

1 HOLD WIRE

Hold the wire with the hand you do not use for writing. If you have trouble gripping the wire, use needle-nose pliers to hold it.

2 PLACE WIRE STRIPPER

Hold the wire stripper in your writing hand. Fit the wire into the appropriate size hole and close the wire stripper ¼"–½" (6mm–1cm) below the end of the wire.

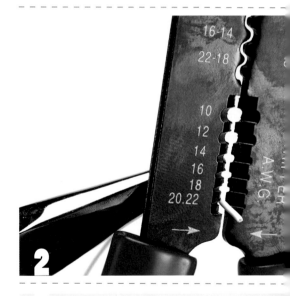

3 STRIP THE WIRE

Pressing firmly, clamp the wire stripper around the wire, then pull the insulation off. The wire cutters cut just the insulation, leaving the wire intact.

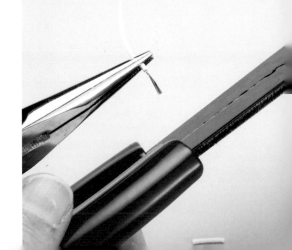

SOLDERING

You will use a technique called *soldering* to connect wires and electronic components. Solder is like hot glue for electronics. It is a metal that is melted with a soldering iron to connect the metal parts of electronics and wires. Electrical solder creates an electrical connection allowing electricity to flow easily from one electronic part to another. You will be soldering for many of the projects, which is great because soldering is a lot of fun. It's very easy to learn how to solder, and we will cover the basics here: what to do when you get a brand-new soldering iron, how to solder, how to keep your soldering iron clean, and what to do if you mess up. Soldering is very hot, so make sure to review all of the safety tips before you get started.

SOLDERING IRON BASICS

Maintaining your soldering iron is the first step in successful soldering. On this page, you'll learn how to prepare a new soldering iron and how to keep it clean.

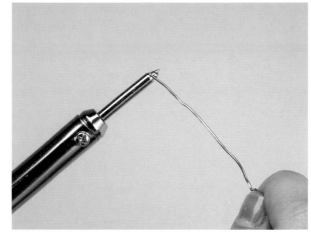

TINNING A NEW SOLDERING IRON TIP

When you buy a new soldering iron, the first thing you need to do is tin the tip. Plug in and turn on the soldering iron, and wait for it to heat up. Once it's heated, hold solder to the tip of the soldering iron. Rotate the soldering iron, applying a thin layer of solder to the entire tip, so the tip is a nice, even silver color.

CLEANING THE SOLDERING IRON

While you're using the soldering iron, the tip may get dirty, especially if you get plastic or too much solder on it. To clean it, wipe the tip on a wet sponge while the iron is still hot.

SOLDERING WIRE

Soldering is all about making a good connection. For most of the projects in this book, you'll make these connections with wires. Here you'll learn how to make a solid electrical connection.

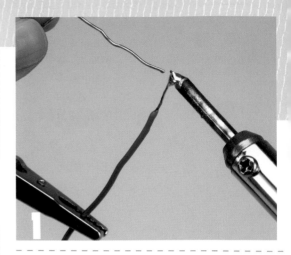

SAFETY TIPS

It is important while soldering to keep the following in mind so that you will have a fun and safe experience:

• Pull back long hair so it doesn't touch the soldering iron. Loose hair or long ponytails can fall onto a hot soldering iron and burn.

• Wear safety glasses and work in a well ventilated area.

• Hold wires with pliers or Helping Hands, not with your real hands. The wires do get hot!

• Never wear loose clothing while soldering. It can fall on the hot soldering iron and catch on fire.

• Always hold the soldering iron by the handle. Never touch the tip of it with your hand.

• Make sure that the metal shaft of the soldering iron never touches anything that can melt or burn.

• When not using the soldering iron, always make sure that the soldering iron rests in its holder.

• Solder over a thick piece of cardboard or a piece of wood. Hot solder can drip or spatter!

• It's great being young, but if you are a young person, it is recommended that you work under parental supervision.

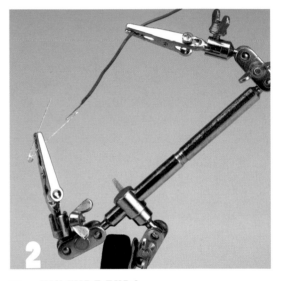

WHY TIN ?

Tinning wire helps to create a good connection between a wire and an electronic part, especially multithreaded wire like headphone wire, used in the *Headphone Hoodie* on page 92.

1 TIN WIRE ENDS

After the wires are stripped, hold the wire with a pair of pliers or clamp. (The wire gets hot!) Hold the tip of the soldering iron to the end of the wire. Hold the solder against the intersection of the soldering iron and wire so that the solder is touching both. When the wire and solder reach the desired temperature, the solder will quickly spread over the tip of the wire.

2 HOLD PIECES IN PLACE

Hold the two pieces that you're connecting so they touch each other. You may need a pair of helping hands— a stand that holds small parts in different positions using clamps.

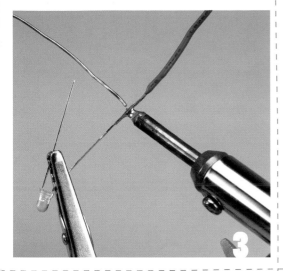

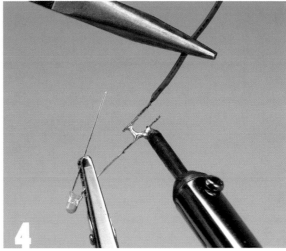

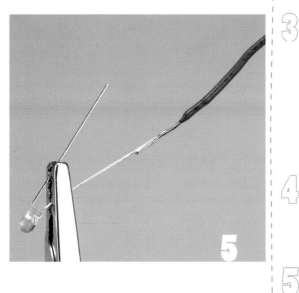

3 APPLY SOLDER

Touch the tip of the soldering iron to the point you would like to connect. Hold the solder so that it is touching the tip of the soldering iron and the connection point at the same time. Once the solder melts, you can use the tip of the soldering iron to spread or move the solder into the desired position.

4 SEPARATE CONNECTION (IF NEEDED)

If you mess up, reheat the connection with the soldering iron to melt the solder, then pull the connection apart.

5 FINISH SOLDERING

The soldering is successful when you have a good strong, neat connection.

WRAP IT UP

Usually when you are finished soldering, you should cover the exposed wire with electrical tape to prevent them from short circuiting or shocking the wearer. All of the soldering projects in this book, however, use a low voltage/current, so covering the wires is not as necessary.

SEWING ELECTRONICS

In the projects in this book, electricity will flow not only through wires but also through thread. Instead of soldering electronics to wire, you will sew them with a special conductive thread that has metal in its very fibers at a molecular level. The electricity flows through the metal in the thread. This section will teach you how to sew two electronic components: LEDs and batteries. You will also use batteries and LEDs in soldering projects.

SEWING LEDS

LEDs are like miniature light bulbs that light up things like the keys of your mobile phone and the power light of your computer. In this book, we'll incorporate LEDs into fashion.

Batteries supply power. You have probably noticed that batteries have a positive/plus (+) and a negative/minus (–) side. This is because electricity flows in a certain direction, from the positive side to the negative side. When connecting certain parts like LEDs, you need to make sure that the electricity flows from the correct side of the battery into the correct side of the LED. The positive side of the battery should be connected to the long anode lead of the LED. The negative side of the battery should be connected to the short cathode lead of the LED. The round LED often has a flat notch on the negative side.

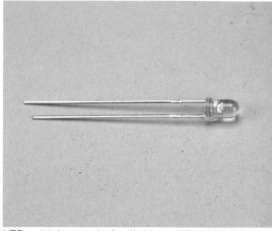

LED, which stands for light-emitting diode

TAKING THE LEAD

Most electronic parts have metal legs called leads. Leads are connected to electricity and are often soldered to wires or the leads of other components.

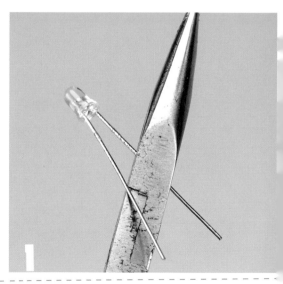

1 CUT LEADS

Cut the leads so that the short lead is ½" (1cm) in length and the long lead is ¾" (2cm) in length.

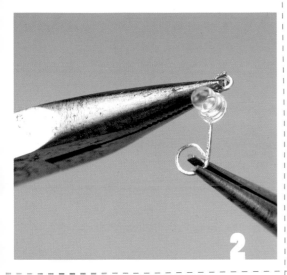

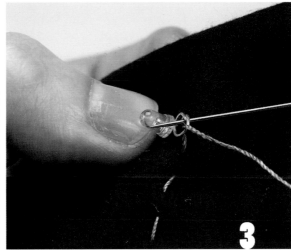

CREATE LOOPS

Use needle-nose pliers to twist the end of each lead toward the LED to create a loop. Always make the loop on the long lead larger; this is connected to the positive side of the battery.

BEGIN SEWING LEAD

With the conductive thread connected to the positive side of the battery and threaded through a needle, insert the needle through the bottom of the large loop of the long lead of the LED. Exit the loop and reinsert the needle through the bottom of the loop without entering the fabric. (This will wrap the thread around the loop an extra time.)

ATTACH LEADS TO FABRIC

Push the needle through the fabric. Knot the thread and cut the excess. Make sure the thread on the positive side of the LED does not touch the negative side. Repeat steps 3–4 using thread from the negative side of the battery to stitch the small loop of the LED. This will connect the negative side of the LED to the negative contact on the battery.

For all of the projects in this book you should use coin cell batteries CR2032 and battery holder BS7.

On the battery holder BS7, the positive side of contact is on the side, and the negative contact is along the bottom.

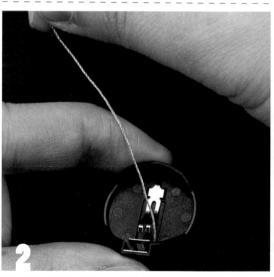

1 REMOVE LEADS

Use pliers to break the leads off the battery holder.

2 BEGIN SEWING POSITIVE CONTACT

Thread a needle with conductive thread; in most cases it will already be attached to the circuit. Push the needle up through the hole under the positive contact of the battery holder.

3 SECURE THE POSITIVE CONTACT

Push the needle back through the hole, looping the thread around the positive connector. Repeat 2–3 times to secure. Knot the thread on the underside of the fabric and cut excess.

4 BEGIN SEWING NEGATIVE CONTACT TO FABRIC

Thread the needle with conductive thread; in most cases it will already be attached to the circuit. Connect to the negative side of the battery by pushing the needle through the fabric and through the slit by the negative contact.

5 FINISH ATTACHING NEGATIVE CONTACT

Push the needle through the hole on the opposite side of the contact, looping the thread around the negative contact. Repeat 2–3 times to secure. Knot the thread on the underside of the fabric and cut the excess.

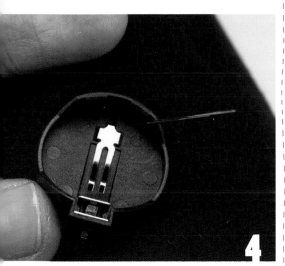

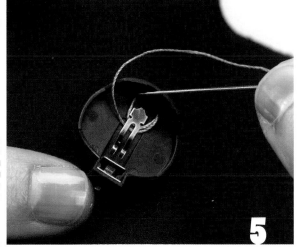

For each part that you have sewn, it is important to test the connection before you insert the battery, to make sure that the electrical connections are secure. If the test does not work, then you can fix your stitches to make them more secure. Make sure that loose conductive threads do not touch parts they are not supposed to touch, and be sure that there is a good, strong connection with lots of thread wrapped around the lead or contact.

TEST SETUP

Using alligator clip jumper wires, connect the positive side of the battery to the positive side of the connection. In this demonstration, we're using LEDs, so the large loop is always the positive connection. Connect the negative side of the battery to the negative connection: the short lead (small loop) of the LED. Only touch the thread with the alligator clip; don't clamp the thread as this could cause it to fray.

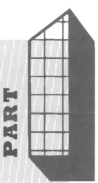

PART 1

ACCESSORIES

In this chapter, we'll explore the worlds of accessories and electronics in two different ways: turning electronics into accessories and making accessories electronic.

Think about it: Every day we carry around electronics—headphones, earbuds, mobile phones, flash drives—so why not make them into fashion accessories? You can do just that! Make earbuds stylish with the *Flowerbud Earbuds* on page 32. Incorporate your headphones into a fashion forward *Monster Music Hat* on page 50. You can even make that flash drive beautiful by turning it into a necklace or bracelet, like *Felt Flower Flash Drive* on page 36.

You'll also learn to make fashion accessories electronic. Rethink the traditional locket and use digital photos to make a *Digital Locket* on page 40. For the *Nightlife Necklace* on page 44, use LEDs instead of gemstones to make jewelry that glows. Even your shoes can get into the action. With *Twinkle Toes* on page 72, you can add super sparkle to shoes that do more than just glitter; they light up with each step.

FLOWERBUD EARBUDS

I grew up in Florida and as a young girl loved picking flowers year round, tucking them behind my ear. I wanted to combine this memory with headphone earbuds to make an accessory that's fun to wear. I hope that wearing these earbuds lets you share in that same girlish fun.

TECHNIQUES

Knotting thread, page 14

Knotting off, page 15

MATERIALS

over-the-ear earphones

craft felt in red, pink, blue and purple

8 black beads

3 yellow beads

6 small white beads

8–10 small orange beads

thread to match bead colors

sewing needle

permanent adhesive (such as Magna-Tac)

scissors

ballpoint pen

flower patterns on page 115

1 TRACE AND CUT FLOWERS

Use a ballpoint pen to trace the poppy pattern twice onto the red craft felt. Place scissors on the inside of the traced line to cut out the two pieces. Repeat for 1 each of pink flower I and pink flower II on the pink craft felt, 1 blue flower on the blue craft felt and 2 purple flowers on the purple craft felt.

2 BEGIN ATTACHING BEADS ON POPPY

Thread the needle with the black thread and knot the thread. Layer the 2 poppy felt pieces perpendicular to each other. From the underside, insert the sewing needle through the center of the petals and pull until the knot meets the felt. Slide a black bead onto the needle and down the thread. Push the needle down through the petals halfway between the bead and the edge of the top petal's side. Pull the thread tight from the underside of the petals to slightly gather the petal.

3 SECURE BEAD

Push the needle back through the center of the petal's underside and the center of the black bead.

4 ATTACH REMAINING BEADS

Slide a black bead onto the needle and down the thread. Push the needle through outside the bead and at the edge of the petal. Pull the thread tight from the underside of the petals to gather the petal. Repeat for the remaining 6 black beads. Knot the thread on the underside of the petals, and cut the excess thread. Use this same technique and orange thread to sew 4–5 orange beads onto each of the pink flowers.

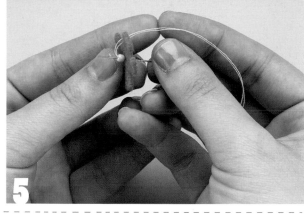

5 SEW FIRST YELLOW BEAD ONTO BLUE FLOWER

Thread the needle with yellow thread, and knot the thread. From the underside, insert the sewing needle through the center of the blue flower. Slide a yellow bead onto the needle and down the thread. Take the thread over the edge of the petal, and insert the needle through the center of the blue flower's underside but not through the bead. Pull the thread tight.

6 SEW REMAINING YELLOW BEADS

Slide a yellow bead onto the needle and down the thread, then repeat the bead attachment sewing as in step 5. Repeat this process to attach the last yellow bead.

7 TIGHTEN THE BEADS

Push the needle through all 3 yellow beads and back through the first yellow bead. Pull to tighten the thread. Push the needle to the underside of the flower. Tighten and knot the thread. Repeat steps 5–7 for both purple flowers, sewing 3 white beads onto each flower. Remember to use white thread for the white beads.

8 ATTACH TO EARBUDS

Use permanent adhesive to adhere three flowers to each earbud in your desired pattern. Add more flowers of your own design if you like.

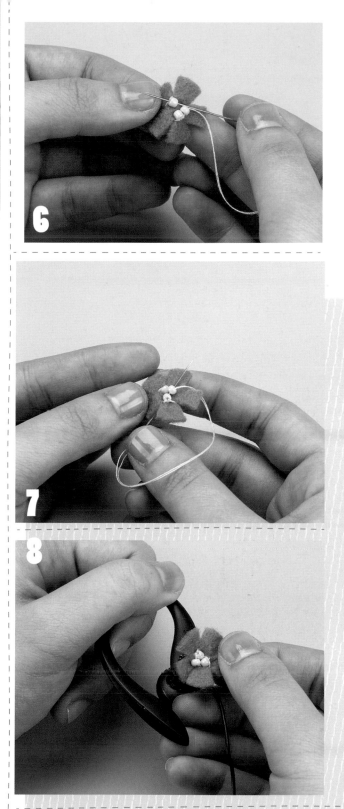

FELT FLOWER FLASH DRIVE

I always carry around my USB flash drive, so that when I see my friends, we can share songs, movies and photos. Then one day I thought, "Wouldn't it be great if the thumb drive were actually an accessory?" With a few pieces of felt and a chain, you can make your USB drive a fabulous part of any outfit.

MATERIALS

USB flash drive with a loop on one end

craft felt in three shades of pink

chain, approximately 22" (56cm) long and with lobster claw clasp

2 jump rings

1½" (4cm) eye pin (available in the jewelry section of craft stores)

hot glue gun, with glue sticks

scissors

needle-nose pliers

ballpoint pen

red fingernail polish (optional)

patterns on page 114

1 CUT PETALS AND ADHERE LARGE PETALS

Trace the patterns on page 114 onto the felt. Use scissors to cut out the petal patterns. Trace and cut the quantity shown on each pattern piece. Use a hot glue gun to adhere the 2 Pattern 1 petals to the flash drive; be careful to not glue the lid.

2 ADD REMAINING PETALS

Use fingernail polish, if desired, to color the end and the lid of the flash drive. Use a hot glue gun to adhere the remaining petals according to the diagram on page 115. Put glue on only the flat side of the petals, and stagger the petals like fish scales for a more flowery look. When you get to the final 4 petals (pattern 5), lay one on each side of the flash drive's loop; be careful not to cover the loop.

3 BEND EYE PIN

Use needle-nose pliers to bend the 1½" (4cm) eye pin in half.

4 WRAP PETAL AROUND EYE PIN

Apply hot glue near the flat edge of one of the Pattern 7 petals. Lay the eye pin into the glue, with the loop sticking out past the flat edge. Apply hot glue to the inside edge of the petal. Tightly wrap the remaining part of the petal around the eye pin.

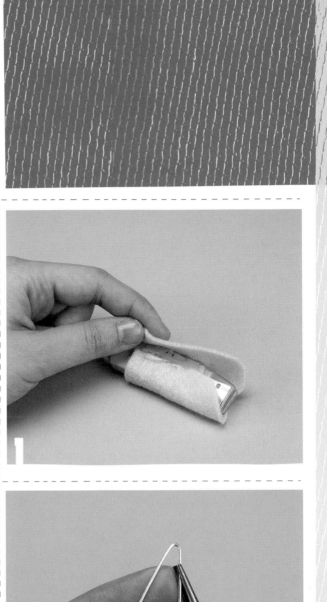

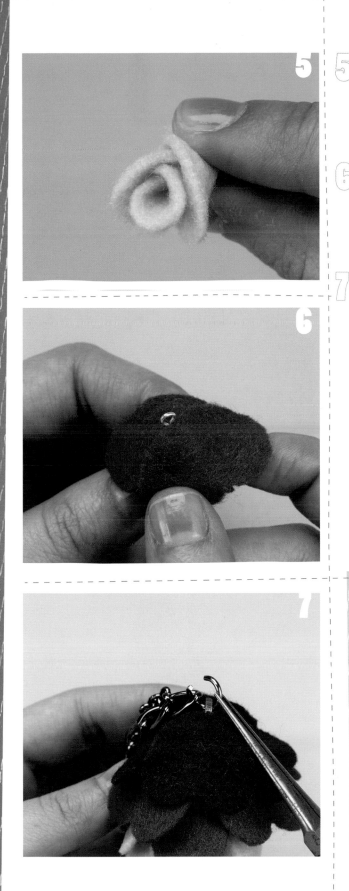

5 ADD 2 PETALS

Apply hot glue to the outer edges of the remaining two Pattern 7 petals, and place slightly below the center petal, attached in step 4. Wrap the 2 outer petals firmly around the center petal.

6 FINISH SMALL FLOWER

Use hot glue to adhere the 4 Pattern 6 petals, layering them onto the flower center from step 5. Be sure to lay the last 2 petals against the eye pin, but don't cover it.

7 ADD FLOWERS TO CHAIN

Use needle-nose pliers to open 2 jump rings. Insert 1 jump ring into the loop of the flash drive then into one of the links in the chain; use pliers to close the jump ring. Insert the second jump ring into the eye pin loop on the small flower then around the chain—not into a link—so that the small flower pendant can slide freely on the chain. Use pliers to close the jump ring.

DIGITAL LOCKET

This is not your grandmother's locket! This modern locket will allow you to view digital photos from your digital camera and mobile phone, from social networks and from e-mails. Just embellish the electronic locket with beads, as shown in this project, upload the photos, then stylishly show off photos of all your friends whenever you like.

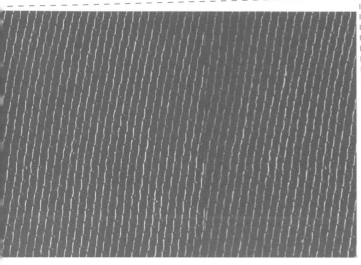

1 PREPARE FRAME

Use needle-nose pliers to open the loop on the digital picture frame; remove the key chain. Use the pliers to close the loop. Load pictures according to the manufacturer's instructions.

2 PLACE FLOWER BEADS

With a photo displayed, place the 4 flower beads on the frame. Be careful not to cover the photo with the flower beads. Use a black marker to trace the outer edge of each flower bead.

3 ATTACH BEADS

Use permanent adhesive to adhere black seed beads onto the frame, on both the front and back. Cover the entire frame except for the frame's function buttons and the spaces marked for the flower beads. You can use larger and smaller beads, as I did here, to create an interesting texture.

4 ATTACH FLOWER BEADS

Use permanent adhesive to adhere the flower beads to the marked spaces on the frame.

5 ATTACH CHAIN

Use needle-nose pliers to open the jump ring. Insert the jump ring into the loop on the digital frame then around the necklace chain, so that the locket can slide freely on the chain. Use the pliers to close the jump ring.

NIGHTLIFE NECKLACE

I wanted to design a necklace that uses LEDs to look like a shiny gemstone, but using a regular LED would look like a flashlight around the neck. For this project I was challenged to come up with a way to make the LEDs glow faintly, to make people wonder if the glow comes from a special type of shiny stone. Like a mobile phone screen, the LEDs are difficult to see in bright sunlight, but they appear super bright in the dark. The solution is to add a photoresistor to control how brightly the LEDs will glow. When the surrounding light is brighter, the LEDs will glow brighter. When the ambient light is dimmer, the LEDs will glow dimmer.

TECHNIQUES

Knotting thread, page 14

Sewing a running stitch, page 14

Knotting off, page 15

Soldering wire, page 24

Testing connections, page 29

Sewing battery holders, page 28

MATERIALS

1–6 small LEDs (size 3mm or T1)

photoresistor

6 pony beads to fit LEDs

1 large bead to fit photoresistor

1 set of alligator clip jumper wires

fine-grit sandpaper

chain, approximately 14" (36cm) long

4 jump rings

2 ribbon crimp ends

lobster claw clasp

conductive thread

battery (CR2032)

battery holder (BS7)

needle-nose pliers

wire cutter

electrical solder

soldering iron

craft and fabric glue (such as Sobo)

½ yard (46cm) of ribbon, 1" (3cm) wide

rotary tool (optional)

domed abrasive point or drill bit (optional)

sewing needle

scissors

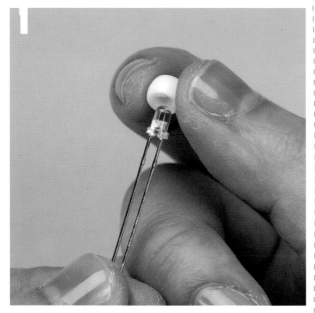

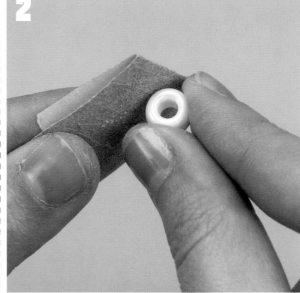

BRIGHT LIGHT

Use six or fewer LEDs in your design. The battery is strong enough to power six LEDs, but more than six lights will result in lights that won't be very bright.

1 TEST FIT

Test to make sure each LED will fit snugly in a pony bead. I used white LEDs and white beads, but feel free to add color and mix it up.

2 SAND BEADS

Use fine-grit sandpaper to sand the outside edges of the pony beads and the large bead to create a matte finish.

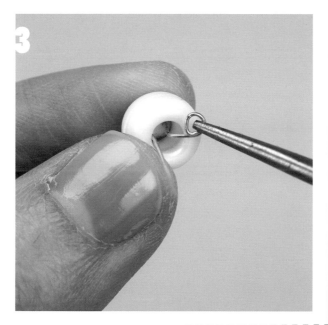

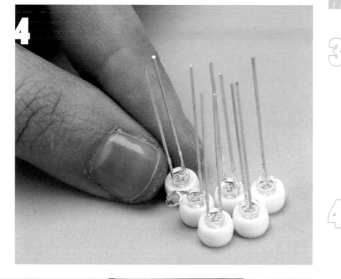

3 INSERT PHOTORESISTOR

Insert the photoresistor into the large bead. If necessary, use the rotary tool and a drill bit or domed abrasive point to widen the opening so the photoresistor will fit. Use a wire cutter to trim ½" (1cm) off 1 of the leads on the photoresistor. Use needle-nose pliers to create a loop on the end of this lead.

4 CREATE DESIGN AND ADD LEDS

Create a design with the pony beads. Insert an LED into each pony bead. Use a wire cutter to cut ½" (1cm) off the short lead of 1 of the LEDs. (For this design, I chose the middle LED on the left, as shown in the photo at left.) Use needle-nose pliers to then create a loop in this shortened lead.

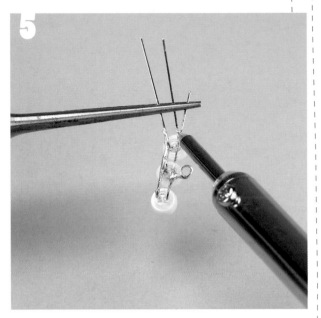

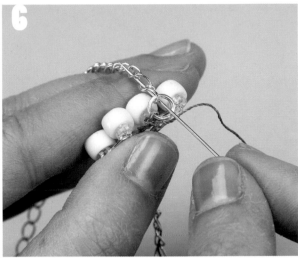

5 ON AND OFF

Put the battery in the holder to turn the necklace on; take the battery out to turn the necklace off.

5 SOLDER LED LEADS AND PHOTORESISTOR

Bend all of the LED leads so that each short lead is touching another short lead and each long lead is touching at least one other long lead (make sure no short lead is touching a long lead). Trim the leads with wire cutters if needed. Use a soldering iron to solder the leads where they touch. Test each connection after you solder it. Add the photoresistor bead and solder the long photoresistor lead to the long lead of the closest LED.

6 ATTACH CHAIN AND ADD CONDUCTIVE THREAD

Cut 2 lengths of chain to the desired length (I cut mine to 7" [18cm] each) using wire cutters. Cut 2 lengths of conductive thread, each of which is double the length from the LEDs to the chain's clasp (in this case about 14" [36cm] each). Tie a knot with 1 length of conductive thread onto the LED lead loop you created in step 4. Secure the knot with a dab of fabric glue, and cut the excess short thread. Test the connection. Attach 1 jump ring to the chain and then to the loop. Thread a sewing needle with the long strand of tied conductive thread, and use the needle to feed the conductive thread through each of the chain's links. Repeat with the second length of conductive thread (threading it through the second chain) and the photoresistor loop you created in step 3.

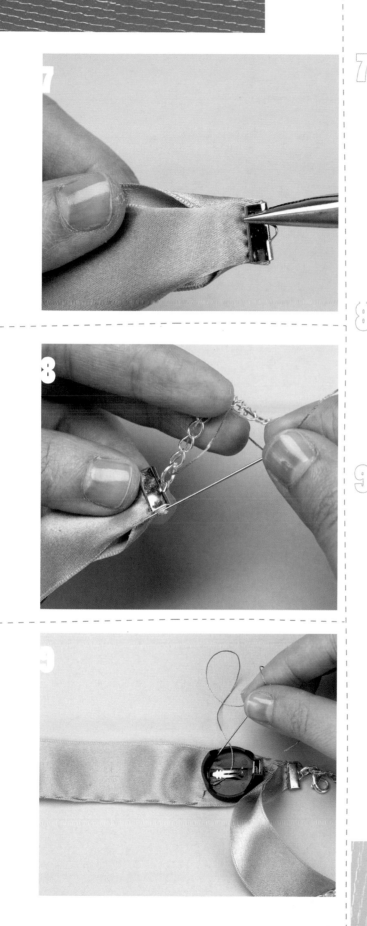

FOLD RIBBON

Use scissors to cut a length of ribbon that when attached to the ends of the necklace will be long enough for you to slide the necklace over your head (I cut mine to 18" [46cm]). Trim the ends at a 45-degree angle to prevent the ribbon from fraying. At 3" (8cm) from 1 end, fold in the sides of the ribbon toward the middle. Fold the ribbon on itself and attach a ribbon crimp end. Make sure a bit of the fold sticks out at the edges of the crimp; you will use this later. Repeat at the other end of the ribbon.

ATTACH RIBBON

Use needle-nose pliers to open 2 jump rings and insert 1 in the loop of each ribbon crimp end. Attach 1 end of each chain onto each jump ring. Insert the needle with the thread from the photoresistor through the fold of ribbon that sticks out of the edge of the ribbon crimp end on that side of the necklace.

ATTACH BATTERY HOLDER

Continuing with the thread from the photoresistor, sew the conductive thread around the positive contact of the battery holder (BS7), being careful to not sew on the extra portion of ribbon that folds over (this portion will cover the battery holder). Repeat the sewing instructions in step 8 with the conductive thread from the LED loop. Sew the conductive thread from the LED loop across the edge of the ribbon to the battery holder. Use this thread to sew around the negative contact of the battery holder. Knot the thead and cut the excess. Attach a lobster claw clasp to the jump ring on one of the crimps.

To wear the necklace, place the ribbon over your head, as shown on page 44, or for a more elegant look, clasp the chains together and let the ribbon loop in the back.

MONSTER MUSIC HAT

Aviator hats (the type that have earflaps) are a perennial winter favorite among the fashion set. So when I saw my friends walking outside in these hats and listening to their portable music players, I thought, "Why not combine the two!" Earflaps are perfect for putting headphones in a hat as they hold the earphones right over the ears for easy listening. I designed my aviator hat to look like a little monster, with earflap paws and a plug-in cord tail.

TECHNIQUES

Knotting thread, page 14

Knotting off, page 15

Sewing a seam allowance, page 16

Backstitching, page 16

Zigzag stitching, page 17

Pinning and cutting patterns, page 18

Turning curves and corners right side out, page 19

MATERIALS

1 yard (91cm) of fleece

craft felt in a contrasting color

thread to match fleece

pins

scissors

sewing machine

small screwdrivers

headphones (not the earbud type)

sewing needle

ribbon or decorative cord (longer than the headphone cord)

tracing paper (optional)

pen (optional)

pliers

patterns on pages 118–119

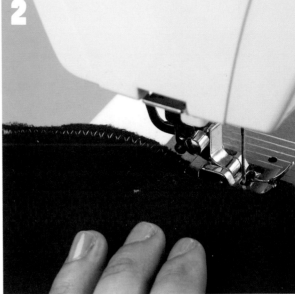

CHOOSING THREAD

Select thread that matches your fleece. I only used a contrasting thread in this demonstration so that you can see the thread clearly as you follow the instructions.

SEAM ALLOWANCE

Use a ⅛" to ¼" (3mm to 6mm) zigzag stitch and a ⅛" (3mm) seam allowance for this project, unless otherwise noted.

1 CUT PATTERN

Pin the patterns to the fleece, and cut out the pattern pieces. Repeat for the felt pattern pieces. Since fleece is very soft and can be hard to work with, you may find it easier to trace the patterns onto tracing paper, pin the traced patterns to the fabric, and then cut out the fabric pieces.

2 BEGIN HAT BODY ASSEMBLY

Pin together 2 pieces of the hat body at the center point. Use a sewing machine to zigzag stitch on the curved portions of the hat pieces, and stop at the center point marked by the pin. Repeat with the 2 remaining hat body pieces. After sewing each piece in this project, trim off the seam allowance close to the stitch line.

CREATE EARS

Lay 1 felt ear piece and 1 fleece ear piece together. Sew around the curved edge. Trim the seam allowance as close to the seam as possible. Turn the ear right side out. Repeat for the other ear. Fold 1 ear onto itself with the felt sides together; pin one edge of the ear about ½" (1cm) from the other edge of that ear. Repeat for the second ear, making sure to fold the second ear the opposite way (i.e., make a mirror image of the first ear) so you have a right ear and a left ear.

CREATE PAWS

Pin 2 of the paw pieces together. Use a zigzag stitch to sew around all sides of the paw, leaving a 1" (3cm) hole at the top of the paw. Turn the paw right side out. Using a straight stitch, sew 2 lines ¾" (2cm) long and 1" (3cm) apart to make toes on the paws. Repeat with the 2 remaining paw pieces.

PIN AND SEW EARS

With 1 piece of the hat body right side up, pin 1 ear 1½" (4cm) from the center point of the hat body and with the folded edge of the ear toward the center point of the hat body. Line up the raw edge of the ear to the edge of the hat body. Because the edge of each ear is straight and the edges of the hat are curved, the open end of the ear might stick out beyond the edge of the hat. That's OK; you can trim this when you are done sewing. Pin the second ear into place on the other side of the center of the hat body. Pin the second piece of the hat body right side down (the side with the seam allowance will be facing up) so that the ears are sandwiched between the hat body pieces. Sew the ears to the hat body using a zigzag stitch and a ⅛" (3mm) seam allowance. If an ear is too thick to go under the presser foot, lift the presser foot as you stitch.

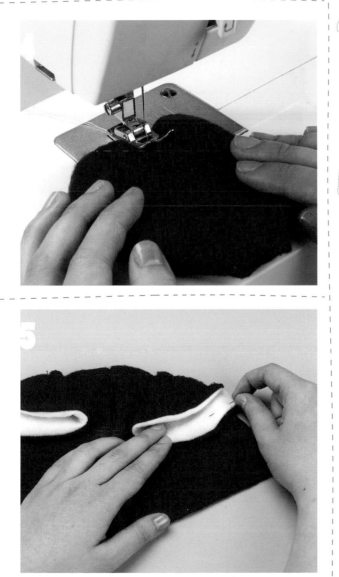

6 DISASSEMBLE HEADPHONES

To disassemble the headphones to expose the speaker and the wires, start by removing the foam covering. Underneath are parts that need to be unscrewed or pried off. Use a set of small electronics screwdrivers and a pair of pliers to remove these parts.

7 PREPARE TO ATTACH HAT BAND

Sew the ends of the hat band together with a zigzag stitch to form a circle. Line up the seam of the hat band with the back seam of the hat body. Pin 1 long edge of the hat band to the bottom edge of the hat body so that the right sides of the hat band and the hat body are together and the hat band is on the outside.

8 PLACE THE HEADPHONES

Place the wires of the headphones in the hat band to prepare for sewing. Place the headphones by the side seams of the hat body and the main cord of the headphones at the back seam.

Pull the cord through the back seam, between the hat body and hat band, so the cord is on the outside of the hat. At the side seams, pull the headphones through to the outside of the hat, keeping the wires inside the hat.

Fold the hat band up to form a trough to hide the headphone wires. Pin the outer edge of the hat band to the inner edge and to the hat body. Stitch the hat band closed and to the hat body with a zigzag stitch. Start and stop sewing at the back seam and the side seams so that you don't sew over any headphone parts or wires.

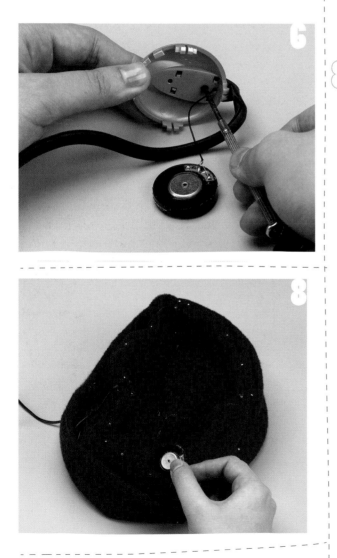

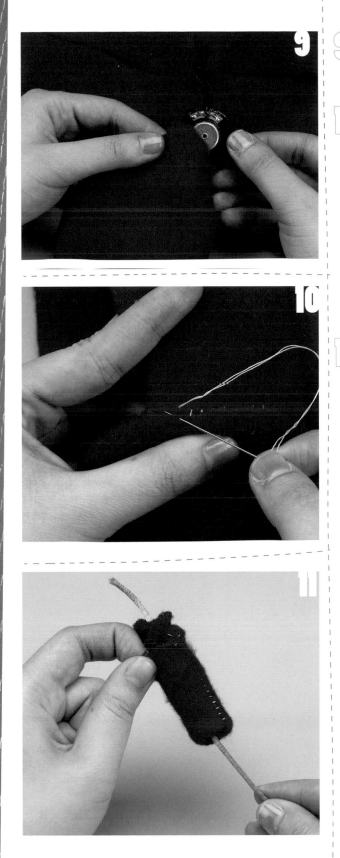

INSERT SPEAKERS

Turn the hat right side out. Insert each headphone speaker into the hole of 1 paw.

ATTACH PAWS

Place the paws where the wearer's ears will be in the hat; extend the bottom of each paw below the hat band. Thread the sewing needle, then knot the thread and stitch the paws in place. When stitching, alternate picking a little bit of fabric up from the paw and a little bit from the hat; this will help hide the stitch. At the top of the paw, fold the open edge of fabric inward and place it over the opening for the cord so that none of the cord is visible from the outside of the hat.

CREATE THE TAIL

Measure the length of the headphone cord that comes out of the back of the hat. Cut a strip of fleece that is 1½" (4cm) wide and the length of the headphone cord. Cut a piece of ribbon or decorative cord that is longer than the strip of fleece. Sew the end of the ribbon to one end of the fleece strip. Fold the strip of fleece lengthwise with the ribbon inside, and sew with a zigzag stitch to form a long tube (be careful not to sew into the ribbon). Pull on the end of the ribbon and push the fleece to turn the tube right side out. Cut off the stitched end of the fleece and ribbon. Thread the headphone cord through the tail and stitch the top of the tail to the back of the hat just like you stitched the paws in step 10.

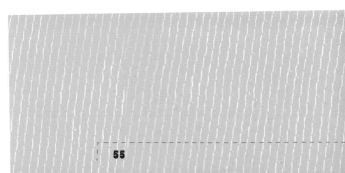

GET-THE-MESSAGE BAG

At parties, I can never hear my mobile phone when it is ringing in my purse. Here is the perfect solution: a bag that lights up when your mobile phone rings. You can use this same technique to make a light-up pocket or purse, or maybe even a light-up jacket (though it won't be machine washable). You'll never miss another call!

MATERIALS

bag with an outside pocket

mobile phone flasher

2 grommets, domed halves only, that fit around the mobile phone flasher

needle-nose pliers

pins

pen

embroidery scissors

permanent adhesive (such as Magna-Tac)

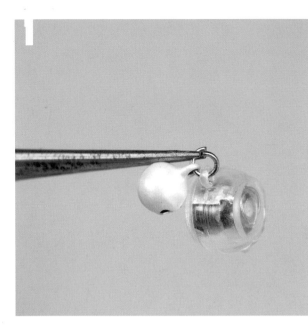

ALL ABOUT MOBILE PHONE FLASHERS

This phone accessory is activated by the mobile phone's frequency, so any nearby mobile phone will activate the flasher when the phone receives or sends a call. You can find mobile phone flashers online and at some stores where mobile phone accessories are sold. Certain types of flashers work for different mobile phones, so check the package before purchasing one.

1 PREPARE MOBILE PHONE FLASHER

Use needle-nose pliers to remove extra pieces from the flasher; leave only the clear device.

2 TRACE GROMMET

Place one round, domed piece of grommet on the outside pocket of the bag, and trace the inside hole of the grommet. Make sure this is a pocket that will keep your phone close to the flasher.

③ CUT GROMMET HOLE

If the pocket is lined, pin the lining to the outside layer of the bag. Use sharp embroidery scissors to cut the traced circle out of the bag pocket. If the bag is lined, be sure to cut the lining, too.

④ ADD MOBILE PHONE FLASHER

Insert the mobile phone flasher into the hole in the bag pocket. Fill the ridges of 1 domed grommet with permanent adhesive. Place the grommet around the flasher. Firmly press the grommet from the outside while tracing the grommet's ridge on the inside of the pocket with your fingers; this will ensure the fabric gets pressed into the ridge and is firmly attached. Use clamps to secure while the adhesive dries. When the glue is dry, fill the ridge of the second domed grommet with adhesive and glue to the inside of the pocket around the flasher. Again, clamp this into place while the glue dries. To use this gadget, place your mobile phone in the pocket and close to the flasher. When your phone rings, the flasher will be activated by the frequency of the phone.

MATERIALS

¼ yard (23cm) of solid pink fabric (or other petal color)

¼ yard (23cm) of patterned pink fabric (or other petal color)

¼ yard (23cm) of green fabric

white fabric approximately 6" x 36" (15cm x 91cm)

7 small LEDs

battery (CR2032)

battery holder (BS7)

conductive thread

sewing machine

iron

scissors

pins

sewing needles

30" (76cm) cord to use as a drawstring

thread to match each of the fabrics

¼ yard (23cm) of ribbon, 2" (5cm) wide (optional)

2 coordinating jingle bells (optional)

patterns on pages 116–117

LIGHT-UP PETAL PURSE

The design for this purse was inspired by traditional Japanese handbags usually made in the shape of flowers or animals. The purse uses the mechanism of the drawstring to light up an LED bead pattern hand embroidered on the purse. When the drawstring is pulled closed, parts of the embroidered pattern touch each other, which closes the circuit and turns on the LEDs. Opening the purse opens the circuit, which turns off the LEDs. Sparkling!

1 PIN AND CUT PATTERN PIECES

Pin and cut out the pattern pieces as follows: small petals from the solid pink fabric; large petals and base top from the patterned pink fabric; purse bases from the green fabric; and top band from the white fabric.

2 SEW BASE TOP

With the base top folded so that the right side of the fabric is inside, use a sewing machine to sew the ends of the base top together with a straight stitch and a ¼" (6mm) seam allowance. Use an iron to press the seam open.

3 ASSEMBLE AND SEW PURSE BASE

Lay 1 purse base piece right side up on the table. Lay the base top right side up onto that purse base piece. Pin these pieces together at the outer edges. Lay the second purse base piece right side down on the base top. Pin the 3 pieces together. Using thread that matches the purse base, sew all 3 layers together with a ¼" (6mm) seam allowance, leaving 1" to 1½" (3cm to 4cm) open so you can turn the purse right side out.

4 TURN THE PURSE RIGHT SIDE OUT

Snip small, evenly spaced (¼" to ½" [6mm to 13mm]) slits around the seam, being careful not to cut the thread. Remove all pins from the assembled purse. Turn the purse right side out. The top should stand up from the purse base.

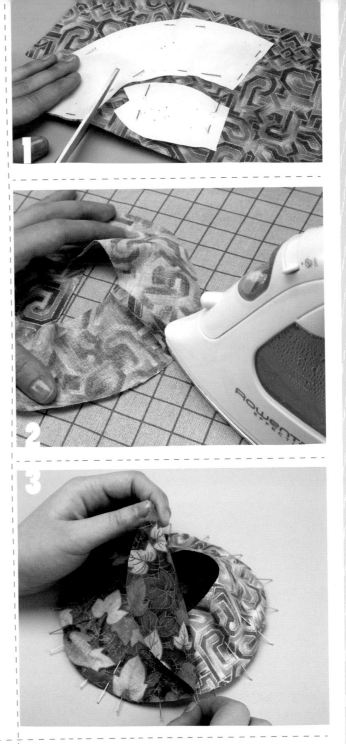

5 CLOSE OPENING IN BASE SEAM

Use an iron to press the edge of the base. Thread a sewing needle with the thread that matches the purse base. Knot the thread, and stitch closed the opening you left in step 3.

6 SEW AND TURN PETALS

Using a sewing machine and thread that matches the fabric, sew all of the petals with right sides together and a ¼" (6mm) seam allowance; leave the bottom of each petal open so you can turn them right side out. Cut off the seam allowance corners of each of the petal points and cut ¼" to ½" (6mm to 13mm) notches around the seam. Cut a notch in the center of the *V* of each petal as well. Turn the petals right side out, and press them with an iron.

7 ASSEMBLE TOP BAND AND MAKE LOOPS IN LED LEADS

Fold one short end of the top band up ¼" (6mm) and carefully use an iron to press the fold in place. Roll the same end up another ¼" (6mm) and press that fold in place. Repeat for the other short end of the band. Fold the band in half lengthwise, and use an iron to press the fold. Before you start embroidering, form loops in the leads on each LED. Create a large loop from the positive lead and a small loop from the negative.

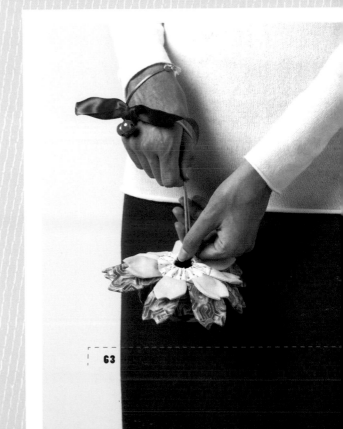

CIRCUIT EMBROIDERY DIAGRAM

_ _ conductive thead connecting to negative lead

_ _ _ conductive thread connecting to positive lead

_____ fold line

▬▬ bottom edge of fabric

COLORED THREAD

The red thread shown in the diagram at right and used in the photos opposite is merely to differentiate the thread going to the positive leads from the thread going to the negative leads. When you do the sewing for this part of the project, all the conductive thread will be the same color.

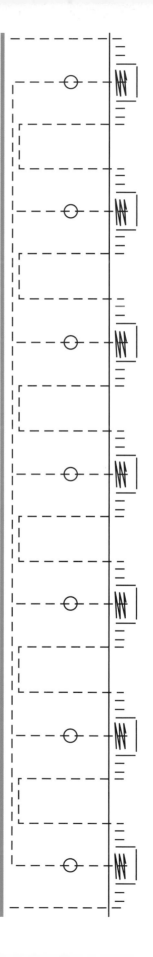

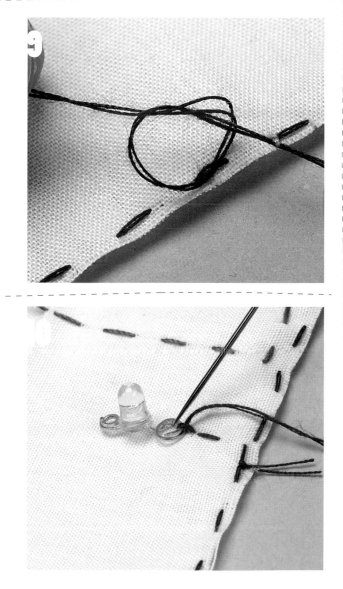

8 STITCH CONDUCTIVE THREAD TO MAKE CIRCUIT ON TOP BAND

Open the top band so that the fold line is in the center and the right side is up. Thread a sewing needle with conductive thread, and knot the thread. Starting at the bottom edge and ½" (1cm) from 1 rolled edge, sew a vertical running stitch to the fold line using conductive thread (represented by the gray thread) that will attach to the negative lead of the battery holder. Leave the thread on the needle for later steps. Thread another sewing needle with conductive thread, and knot the thread. Starting ½" (1cm) in from the line just sewn, sew along the bottom edge of the top band a horizontal line of running stitches of conductive thread (represented by the red thread for instructional purposes only) that will attach to the positive lead of the battery holder. Stop stitching the positive-lead thread 1" (3cm) from the other rolled side edge. Leave the thread on the needle for later steps.

9 SEW POSITIVE PART OF CIRCUIT

The positive part of the circuit (represented by the red thread) will connect the positive side of the battery to the positive leads of the LEDs. The positive leads will all be attached to the conductive thread sewn across the bottom edge of the top band. Thread yet another sewing needle with conductive thread, then ½" (1cm) from the negative (gray) line, tie the end of the thread onto the positive (red) line.

10 ATTACH FIRST LED

With the threaded needle from step 9, sew a couple of stitches toward the fold and attach the large loop of 1 LED. Tie a knot in the thread, and cut the thread close to the knot. Knot the thread left on the needle, and sew the small loop of the LED onto the top band. Continue sewing a running stitch until you reach the fold. Bring the needle to the front side of the fabric just above the fold.

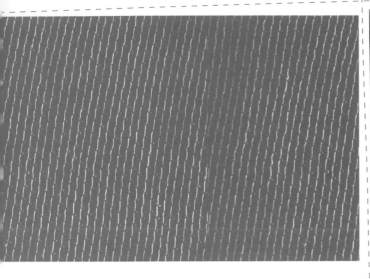

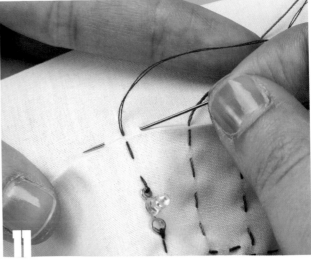

⅂⅂ SEW POSITIVE CONTACT

Bring the needle to the side and create a few horizontal stitches (top image). Then bring the needle out at the fold line, and create a vertical stitch to hold the horizontal stitches in place (middle image). Continue sewing the positive circuit stitches as shown on the diagram on page 64.

⅂2 SEW NEGATIVE PART OF CIRCUIT

Using the first needle from step 8, stitch the negative pattern (the black circuit on the diagram on page 64). Above the fold line you will create the negative contacts that will touch the positive contacts when the drawstring is closed; this will make the LEDs turn on. Sew a few vertical stitches then stitch up and around the positive contact, making sure the negative-circuit thread does not touch the positive-circuit thread.

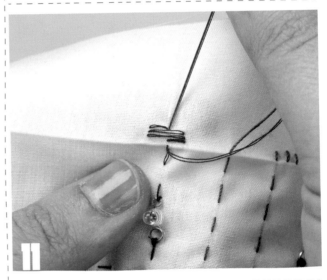

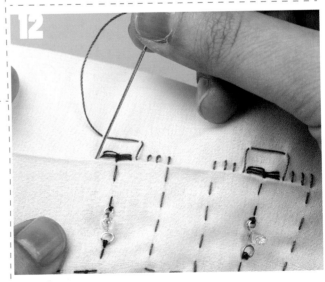

13 ADD DRAWSTRING

Fold the top band over the 30" (76cm) drawstring cord. Thread a sewing needle with white thread. Knot the thread, and sew a running stitch through the front and back of the top band and under the drawstring cord to create a tight channel for the cord. (Don't make the channel too tight; the fabric must be able to slide along the cord for the drawstring effect.)

14 SEW PETALS TO PURSE

Lay the open ends of the large petals against the top edge of the purse and pin them into place. Repeat with the small petals on top of the large petals. Use the sewing machine to sew both layers of petals to the purse; use a ¼" (6mm) seam allowance. Pin the top band with the embroidered pattern face down onto the top row of petals. Use the sewing machine and a ¼" (6mm) seam allowance to stitch the top band to the purse.

15 ATTACH BATTERY HOLDER

Thread two needles with conductive thread. Instead of knotting the thread, tie the end of one to the negative thread in the hand sewn pattern, and the end of the other to the positive thread in the hand sewn pattern. Use a running stitch to stitch both threads down to the base of the purse. Sew the battery holder to the inside of the base, connecting the positive side to the positive contact and the negative side to the negative contact.

16 ADD TRIM

Knot together the ends of the cord. If you like, add a bit of trim to decorate the knot. Cut a piece of ribbon, and trim each end at an angle. Tie the ribbon over the knot. Hand stitch jingle bells onto the ribbon.

EL WIRE SHOES

Inspired by the colorful sneakers of Japanese hip-hop designers at Bathing Ape, I wanted to make sneakers that had the effect of a tricked-out car with neon lights underneath. Thanks to Nike Air shoes, we often see sneaker soles with clear designs to show the air cushioning. By combining the clear tube style of Nike Air with EL wire, you can mod your sneakers for that same under-the-car glow.

MATERIALS

sneakers with a solid, continuous sole (so there won't be any bumps when you attach the EL wire)

2 5' (152cm) lengths of EL wire (this project uses the angel-hair thickness, but you can choose your own)

2 drivers and batteries (available in clip version)

wire cutter

5' (152cm) of polyvinyl clear tubing, less than ½ " (1cm) in diameter

hot glue gun, with glue sticks

scissors

1 CUT POLYVINYL TUBING

Cut the polyvinyl clear tubing in half lengthwise so that each half remains 5' (152cm) long. It may help to cut the top first and then cut the bottom.

2 START GLUING EL WIRE

Using a hot glue gun, start gluing 1 length of the EL wire to the top of the sole at the heel of 1 of the sneakers. Begin with the part of the EL wire that connects to the plug. Place the EL wire on the sole and dab the EL wire with glue.

3 GLUE EL WIRE AROUND SHOE

Continue to glue the EL wire to the sole.

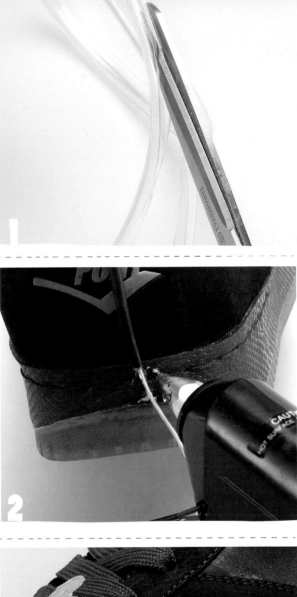

4 FINISH GLUING EL WIRE, THEN CUT EXCESS WIRE

Wrap the EL wire around the shoe a second time, gluing as you go. When you get back to the heel, glue the wire near the starting point, then cut the excess wire with a wire cutter.

5 GLUE POLYVINYL TUBE

Starting at the heel, use a hot glue gun to put glue on the EL wire then press 1 piece of the polyvinyl tubing over the EL wire. Glue a small section at a time, allowing the glue to set before moving on to the next section. For a cleaner appearance inside the tubing, pop any bubbles in the glue.

6 FINISH GLUING TUBING

When you get back to the heel, cut off any extra length of tubing. Repeat steps 2-6 for the second shoe. When you wear these shoes, plug the EL wire into the drivers, and then clip the drivers onto your socks. You can let the drivers show, or you can hide them under the legs of long pants.

MATERIALS

high-heel shoes

2 pedometers

small screwdriver to fit screws in pedometer

2 batteries (CR2032)

2 battery holders (BS7)

2 sets of alligator clip jumper wires

10 LEDs

duct tape

needle-nose pliers

2 breath-strip containers to match ribbon

4' (122cm) of ribbon, 2" (5cm) wide

rotary tool

cutoff wheel rotary tool accessory

sanding disc rotary tool accessory

soldering iron

electrical solder

hot glue gun, with glue sticks

conductive thread

microsuede

glitter

craft and fabric glue (such as Sobo)

wide paintbrush (for glue)

wire

wire cutter

permanent adhesive (such as Magna-Tac)

sewing needle

scissors

pattern on page 114

TWINKLE TOES

I love things that sparkle. And what could be more sparkly than lights? These shoes not only glitter but they also have LLDs that turn on and off. They're super sparkly and they twinkle! What could be better?

What controls the twinkling? A pedometer that you'll hack. It gets connected to the LEDs so that every time you take a step, the LEDs turn on and off. You'll twinkle while you walk!

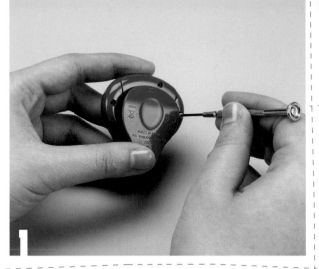

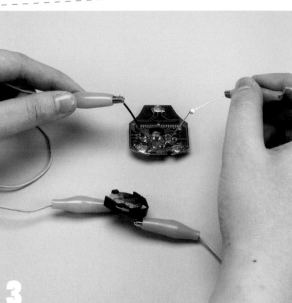

OPEN PEDOMETER

Use a screwdriver to remove the screws from the back of the pedometer.

UNSCREW BOARD

Use a screwdriver to remove the screws from the interior board. Remove from the board all items except for the lever and the spring.

TEST CONNECTIONS

With the alligator clip jumper wires, connect the positive side of the battery to the long leg of an LED. Connect the other jumper wires to the negative side of the battery and a piece of wire. Tape the pedometer lever in the down position to complete the connection to the board contacts. Find the lever leads so you can use the lever as a switch. Start by flipping the board over; find the leads that are connected to the board by touching the LED lead and the wire to the board parts. Continue to test the contact points until the LED lights up. After you find the 2 contact points, put the lever in the open position. Retest the connection; the LED should not light up.

MATCH POINT

With the lever side up, look closely at the board to see where the wires are placed for the spring and the lever. This will help you quickly find the contact points on the other side of the board.

OPEN BREATH-STRIP CONTAINER

Remove the label from the breath-strip container. With your hands, pry the container apart at the side seams

CUT PEDOMETER BOARD TO SIZE

Use needle-nose pliers to hold the board. Use the cutoff wheel attachment for the rotary tool to cut the pedometer board to fit inside the bottom of the breath-strip container. If an edge is ragged, use a sanding disc for the rotary tool to smooth the edge. Place the board with the lever side up in the bottom of the strip container. Make sure the lever can bounce up and down. (See detail shot below.)

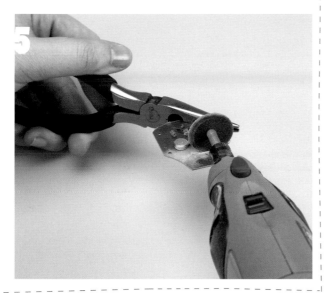

Resized board in bottom of breath-strip container

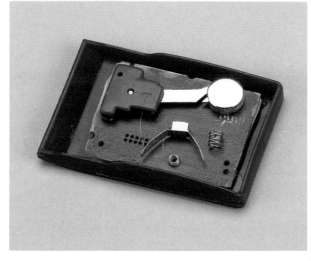

SOLDER WIRE

Measure wire so it connects to the connection points (found in step 3) on the pedometer board and reaches across the board and extends another ¾" (2cm). Cut 2 pieces of wire to this length. Strip each wire ½" (1cm) on one end. On the other end of each wire, strip a very small amount; tin that end. Use a soldering iron to attach the tinned end of 1 wire to 1 connection point, allowing the remaining wire to stick out past the edge of the strip container. Repeat for the second wire, soldering it to the second connection point. Use a hot glue gun to cover each solder connection plus ⅛" (3mm) of wire; this will help secure the connections.

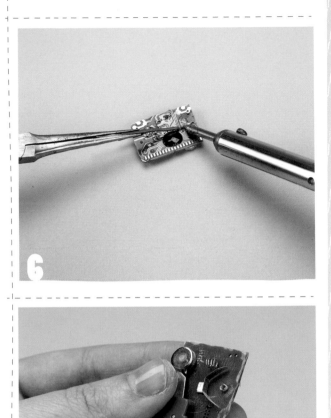

MAKE LOOPS

Use small needle-nose pliers to create a loop in each exposed wire end; these will stick out of the end of the strip packet.

ADD COVER

In the top of the container, cut 2 slits for the wires to fit through when the container is closed. Place the board with the lever facing down in the top of the container and with the wires sticking through the slits. Close the container.

ATTACH CONDUCTIVE THREAD

Cut 2 pieces of conductive thread, each 18"
(46cm) long. Tie 1 length of conductive thread
to each wire loop that was made in step 7.
Make sure each length of conductive thread
touches only 1 wire loop. Apply a dab of fabric
glue to each knot, then cut off the short tail of
thread extending from each knot.

COVER CONTAINER WITH RIBBON

Cut enough ribbon to cover the breath-strip
container. Push needles with conductive thread
through the ribbon. Apply fabric glue to
the entire surface of the ribbon. Place the
container vertically on the ribbon. Fold the
ribbon's sides in, as though you were wrapping
a gift. Keep the conductive threads and the
ribbon taut. Use duct tape to secure ribbon.
Push the needle through the ribbon on the
side of the pack. Use a running stitch, and
exit at the other end.

THREAD CONDUCTIVE THREAD
THROUGH RIBBON

Cut a length of ribbon that will cover the inside
of the shoe's heel, loop over the pedometer
assembly plus ½" (1cm) and loop back
over the heel. (I cut a 7" [18cm] length of
ribbon.) Find the halfway point and adhere the
pedometer pack to the ribbon with fabric glue.
Make sure to place the pedometer pack so the
lever is in the open position. You can test this
by shaking the pedometer pack up and down
and listening for the lever's movement. Allow
the glue to dry. Sew each conductive thread
through the ribbon on each side, creating a
line of running stitches about ½" (1cm) long
through one layer of the ribbon only. Make
sure the threads come out on the backside
of the ribbon.

12 ATTACH RIBBON TO SHOE

Apply fabric glue to 1" (3cm) of the inside ends of the ribbon. Fold the ribbon in half. Apply fabric glue to the inside of the shoe's heel. Press the side of the ribbon without the pedometer pack onto the glue. Use the pattern to cut a heel piece from the microsuede. Apply fabric glue to the microsuede heel piece, and press it onto the ribbon inside the shoe.

13 SOLDER LEDS

Lay the LEDs in a desired pattern. Use a soldering iron to attach the LEDs. Solder short leads to other short leads and long leads to other long leads. Bend 1 of the short leads and 1 of the long leads into small loops for sewing later. Use a piece of colored thread or marker to mark which loop is connected to the long leads and which is connected to the short leads. Test the connections by using alligator clip jumper wires to connect the negative side of the battery to a short LED lead and the positive side to a long lead. If the LEDs light up, you've soldered good connections. If some of the LEDs do not light up, check their connections to make sure the short leads are all touching other short leads, and the long leads are all touching other long leads.

14 ADHERE LEDS TO SHOE

Insert one 18" (46cm) length of conductive thread through each loop from step 13. Tie a knot in each of the threads. Apply a dab of fabric glue to each knot, and cut off the short tail of thread extending from each knot. Test the connection by touching the jumper wires to the thread and the battery. Use needle-nose pliers to gently bend and shape the LED leads to fit the shoe's shape. Don't grip directly on any of the soldered connections. Use permanent adhesive to adhere the LED design to the shoe. If any of the parts are sticking up, apply another dab of adhesive.

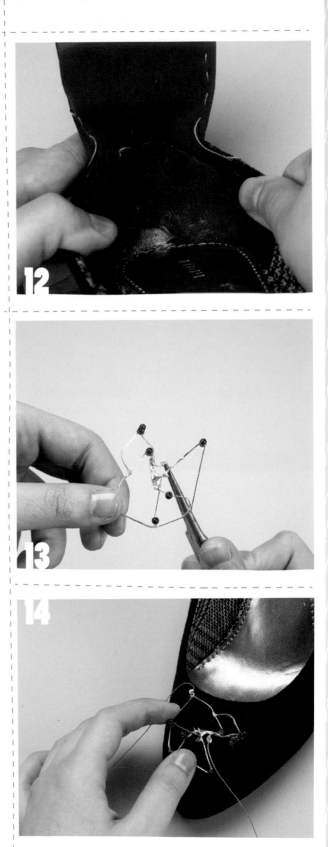

15 CONNECT CONDUCTIVE THREADS

Push a needle threaded with conductive thread through both layers of ribbon so the thread comes out at the back of the ribbon.

Keeping threads loose enough to run along the side of the shoe, tie a knot with the conductive thread from the short LED lead and the conductive thread from the ribbon on the same side of the shoe. Use fabric glue to adhere the conductive thread to the outside of the shoe.

16 CONNECT BATTERY

Thread the conductive thread from the ribbon into a needle. Make sure the thread reaches to the battery that will sit on the inside of the high heel. Insert the needle into the hole on the back of the battery holder, under the negative contact, and through the second hole on the battery holder. Repeat 2 or 3 more times to secure. Tie a knot in the thread on the back of the battery holder, and cut the thread. Apply a dab of fabric glue to secure the knot. Repeat the process using the thread from the positive lead of the LEDs and the positive contact on the battery. Use a hot glue gun to adhere the battery holder to the inside of the heel. Use fabric glue to adhere the conductive thread along the sides of the shoe.

17 ADD GLITTER AND RIBBON

Use a paintbrush to apply a thin layer of fabric glue in small sections to the outside of the shoe. Add a thick layer of glitter to the glue. Cut a length of ribbon that's long enough to wrap around your ankle once—more times, if desired—and to tie a bow of the size desired. The ribbon shown on page 72 is 38" (97cm) long. Insert the batteries when you're ready to wear the shoes.

SPRINKLING GLITTER

When sprinkling the glitter, place a box lid under the shoe to collect the excess. This excess glitter can be reused; just funnel it back into the bottle.

RAIN, RAIN GO AWAY

These are fair-weather shoes. The batteries and glue won't hold up to water.

2 CLOTHING

High-tech fashion is appearing on runways more and more as designers use technology in luxury products. Maybe you remember the EL wire jacket that Kanye West wore to the GRAMMYs. Tech fashion is becoming a part of companies like Versace, which has a research and development team devoted to the area, and Burton, which produces a snowboarding jacket that can play music.

Now you can be on the cutting edge by making your own tech fashions. In this section you'll learn to sew conductive thread into a hoodie so that you can listen to music in its hood. You'll add to a jacket buttons that light up when the jacket is buttoned. Finally, you'll learn to make your own EL wire-lit fashion as you work on the *Lightning Bug Costume* (page 98). Soon every day will be your own tech fashion show!

BLOOMING BUTTONS

The perfect detail to add to any coat or jacket, blooming buttons light up when the garment is buttoned and turn off when it is unbuttoned. The buttons in this project use a reed switch, which turns on when it is near a magnet.

TECHNIQUES

Knotting thread, page 14

Sewing a whipstitch, page 15

Knotting off, page 15

Soldering wire, page 24

MATERIALS

jacket or sweater with buttons

small reed switches, 1 for each button on jacket

LEDs, 1 for each button on jacket

plastic container from gum ball machine, 1 for each button on jacket

metal button or disk (must be magnetic), 1 for each button on jacket

battery (CR2032), 1 for each button on jacket

rare earth magnet with a hole through the center, 1 for each button on jacket

battery holder (BS7), with leads attached, 1 for each button on jacket

craft knife

quarter

pen

craft felt (to match LEDs)

scissors

hot glue gun, with glue sticks

sewing needle

thread (to match jacket)

3 sets of alligator clip jumper wires

sandpaper

electrical solder

soldering iron

scrap fabric or paper towel

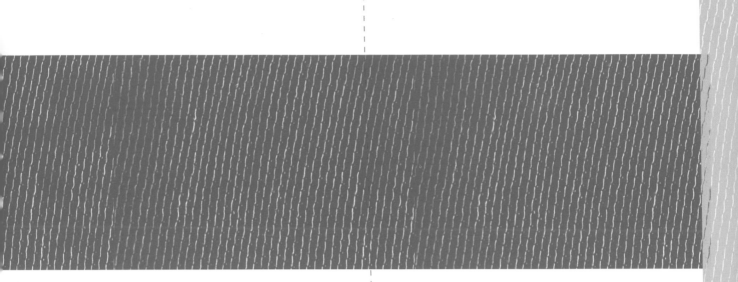

1   TEST REED SWITCHES

Using alligator clip jumper wires, connect the positive side of a battery to the long lead of 1 LED. Connect the short lead of the LED to 1 reed switch. Connect the reed switch to the negative side of the battery. Hold 1 earth magnet near the reed switch, and see if the LED lights up. If the LED does not light up, you may need to buy a new reed switch.

2   ATTACH METAL BUTTON AND REED SWITCH TO BATTERY HOLDER

Use glue from a hot glue gun to adhere 1 metal button or disk to the bottom of 1 battery holder. Lay 1 reed switch across the metal button; be careful to make sure that none of the metal parts of the reed switch touch the metal button. The reed switch needs to be able to touch the lead of the battery holder and the lead of an LED when the LED is laid across the metal button. If the reed switch is too long, trim the ends. For soldering, hold the parts in place with a piece of fabric or a paper towel—the parts will get hot! Solder the reed switch to the negative lead of the battery holder.

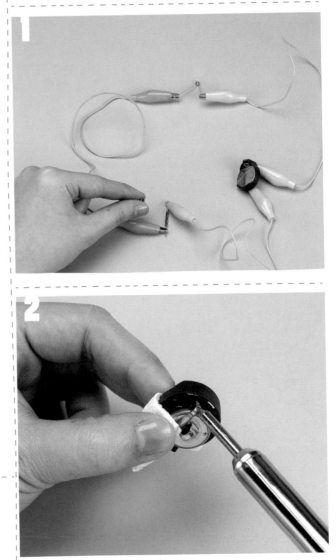

CONNECT LED

Bend the leads of 1 LED to fit around the side of the battery holder from step 2. (See detail shot at left for LED placement.) The LED should rest just above the center of the battery. Solder the LED's long lead to the positive lead of the battery holder. Solder the LED's short lead to the open end of the reed switch.

SAND CONTAINER

Use fine-grit sandpaper to sand the inside and outside of 1 plastic container. This will diffuse the LED light and create a nice glow.

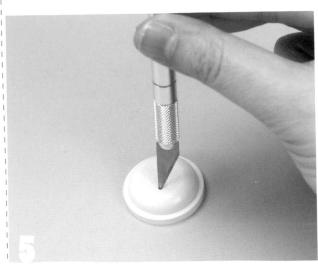

5 CREATE BUTTON

Use a craft knife to create 2 small holes in the lid of the plastic container from step 4 by gently twisting the point of the craft knife into the lid.

6 ATTACH RARE EARTH MAGNET TO JACKET

Thread a sewing needle with thread that matches the jacket, and knot the thread. Sew the rare earth magnet onto the inner edge of 1 buttonhole by inserting the needle through the hole of the magnet then through the fabric. Repeat 3 or 4 times. Knot the thread, then cut the thread near the knot.

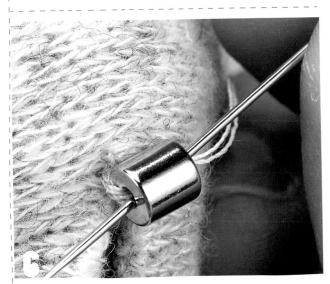

7 WIDEN BUTTONHOLE

Use scissors to cut the fabric of the jacket to widen the buttonhole from step 6 to accommodate the gum ball container (to about 2" [5cm]). Whipstitch the raw edge of the buttonhole extension to keep it from unraveling.

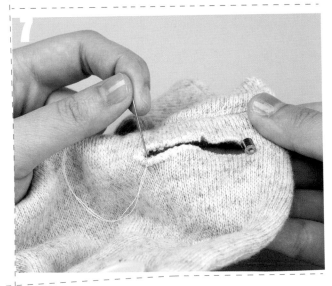

8 ATTACH PETALS

To create petals, use a pen to trace a quarter onto a piece of craft felt, then cut out the circles. Repeat 7 times to make 8 petals total. Use glue from a hot glue gun to attach 2 layers of 4 petals each to the lid of the plastic container. Avoid covering the buttonholes you created in step 5. Don't apply glue to the inside of the lid or the domed part of the container, or you won't be able to open the container.

9 ATTACH BUTTON

Remove the existing buttons from the jacket. Use a needle and thread to attach the lid button from step 8 to the coat in one of the original button's place.

10 ATTACH LIGHT

Place the light assembly from step 3 into the sanded plastic container; the LED should face the inside of the dome. Snap the container and light onto the lid button from step 9. Repeat steps 2–10 for each of the buttons.

To turn on the lights, button the jacket so that the reed switch in each button is near the rare earth magnet on its buttonhole.

SHIRT CIRCUIT

In this project you will sew onto a shirt a circuit made from a battery, conductive thread, and an LED. Most circuits must be etched on a circuit board, but with conductive thread they can be sewn. To light up the LED on this shirt, simply insert a battery into the battery holder. Once you learn to sew with conductive thread, the possibilities for personalizing light-up apparel are endless!

VARIATION

MATERIALS

T-shirt

LED

battery holder (BS7)

battery (CR2032)

2 sheets of tracing paper

conductive thread

pins

pen

sewing machine

sewing needle

scissors

needle-nose pliers

1 TRACE DESIGN

Use a pen to trace the "fashion geek" pattern (see page 121) onto 1 sheet of tracing paper.

2 PIN DESIGN TO SHIRT

Place the traced design on the shirt in the desired position. Place another piece of tracing paper inside of the shirt and underneath the design. Pin through the top layer of tracing paper, the shirt, and the bottom layer of tracing paper. Place pins above and below the traced design to keep the fabric from slipping between the sheets of tracing paper.

3 SEW DESIGN

Using conductive thread and a sewing machine, start a straight stitch at the bottom of the *f* in *fashion*; leave very long tails of thread. Follow the design to the first top notch of the *i* in *fashion*. Cut the thread; leave long tails of thread. Leaving long tails of thread again, start to straight stitch on the second part of the *i* in *fashion*. Continue to straight stitch until you have sewn the complete design. Leave long tails when you cut the thread.

DOUBLE DUTY

Usually you would need a resistor to prevent LED burnout (like if you were using a 9 volt battery). But in these projects we use a battery with less power; the condutive thread helps, too, as it has a lot of resistance.

4 REMOVE PAPER

To remove the tracing paper, place 1 or 2 fingers against some stitches and use the other hand to pull off the tracing paper. Work on small sections of paper, and remove all of the paper from both sides of the shirt. Be sure to pick out any small pieces of paper by the stitches.

5 ATTACH LED

Create a loop in each lead of the LED, making a larger loop with the long (positive) lead. Place the LED where you want the dot for the *i* to go; align the larger lead loop on the *ion* side.

On the left side of the *i* in *fashion*, insert the conductive thread tail from the front of the shirt into a needle, and push the needle through the fabric to the inside of the shirt. Insert the thread tail from the same place on the inside of the shirt into the same needle. Push the thread through the inside of the left small lead loop. Reinsert the needle through the bottom of the loop without entering the fabric (this will wrap the thread around the loop an extra time). Stitch the thread to the inside of the shirt; knot the thread and cut off the excess. Repeat with the conductive thread on the right side of the *i* in *fashion* and the large lead loop on the right side.

6 ATTACH BATTERY HOLDER

Insert the conductive thread tail from the front of the shirt where the partial *g* ends into a needle, and push the needle through the fabric to the inside of the shirt. Insert the thread tail from the same place on the inside of the shirt into the same needle. (You will use this to sew on the positive contact of the battery holder.) Lay the battery holder on the shirt to complete the *g* in *geek*; the positive side of the battery holder should be next to *eek*. Sew the positive contact. Insert the conductive thread tail from the front of the shirt by the *f* in *fashion* into a needle, and push the needle through the fabric to the inside of the shirt. Insert the thread tail from the *f* on the inside of the shirt into the same needle. Sew the negative contact. Insert the battery to wear.

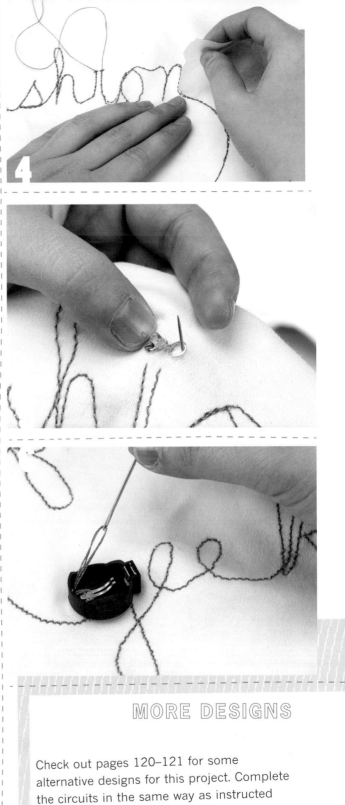

MORE DESIGNS

Check out pages 120–121 for some alternative designs for this project. Complete the circuits in the same way as instructed here for the "fashion geek" design.

HEADPHONE HOODIE

Forget wearing headphones! The *Headphone Hoodie* lets you listen to music when you wear the hood; the speakers are inside the hood, and the wires are replaced by conductive thread. Sports companies have sold some hoodies like this, but they tend to be expensive and available only in limited styles. So why not make your own? It's fun and cheap, and you can make whatever style works for you.

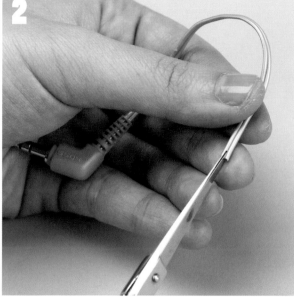

EYELET TOOL KITS

Setting eyelets is easy when you have the proper tools. An eyelet tool kit can help immensely because the tool is perfectly shaped to fit the tube end of the eyelet. You can find these kits in the scrapbooking or paper craft section of a craft store.

CUT FELT ADORNMENTS

Use the patterns to cut 1 heart, 1 small flower and 4 large flowers from craft felt. Use an eyelet tool kit to add an eyelet to the heart where indicated on the pattern.

CUT HEADPHONE WIRES

Cut the headphone wires 5" (13cm) from the plug. Use sharp scissors to clip between the 2 wires that are still attached to the plug. Use your fingers to pull a 1½" (4cm) length of wire apart.

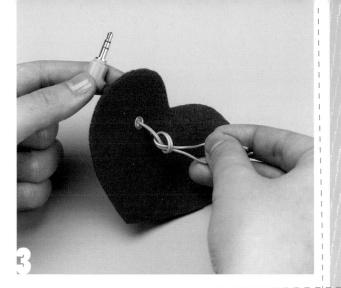

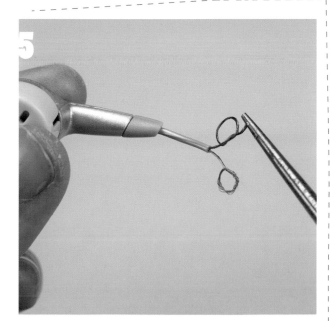

THREAD WIRES THROUGH HEART

Thread the plug's wires through the eyelet on the heart. The plug should be on the front, where the eyelet is smooth, and the split wires should be on the back, where the eyelet was pushed down. Tie a knot in the unsplit section of wire at the back of the heart. This will help secure the plug so that when you pull it out of your music player, you won't rip out the stitches that secure the heart to the hoodie.

STRIP WIRES AND CREATE LOOPS

Strip 1" (3cm) of the split wire. Use wire strippers to do this so that you don't cut the interior wires. You may need to do this in small sections. Separate the wires by color. Use needle-nose pliers to twist wires of the same color together, and form 1 small loop of each color.

PREPARE EARPHONE WIRES

Cut each earphone wire 1½" (4cm) below the earphone. Strip 1" (3cm) of each wire. Separate the wires by color. Use needle-nose pliers to twist wires of the same color together, and form 1 small loop of each color.

6 TIN THE LOOPS

Tin all the loops you created in steps 4 and 5. Audio wires are stranded, meaning they have many small wires. Once you tin them, the solder will connect all of the small wires to make them like 1 thick wire. Tinning may take a bit of finesse, as there might be small fibers mixed in with the wires that melt to the solder.

7 SEW CONDUCTIVE THREAD THROUGH HOODIE

Try on the hoodie, put the hood up, and mark where your ears are for headphone placement. Make sure these marks are even with each other. Cut 4 lengths of conductive thread: 2 segments should reach from the hoodie's left pocket to the left ear mark plus an additional 12" (30cm); the other 2 should reach from the hoodie's left pocket, toward the left ear mark, across the base of the hood, and to the right ear mark plus an additional 12" (30cm).

Thread 1 pocket-to-left-ear piece of conductive thread into a needle. Start sewing a running stitch just above the pocket and on the inside of the hoodie, parallel to the zipper. Leave a 6" (15cm) tail by the pocket. Be sure to make shallow stitches so the conductive thread doesn't show on the outside of the hoodie. Continue the running stitch until you reach the mark for the left ear. Repeat this with the remaining pocket-to-left-ear segment, sewing a running stitch parallel to the first but ¼" (6mm) away.

Repeat this with the 2 pocket-to-right-ear pieces of conductive thread, starting at the left pocket, running parallel to the 2 pocket-to-left-ear conductive threads, but then going across the base of the hood and to the right ear mark.

LOUD AND CLEAR

Whenever you rework audio wires, you have to tin them so you'll get a clear connection. See more about tinning on page 24.

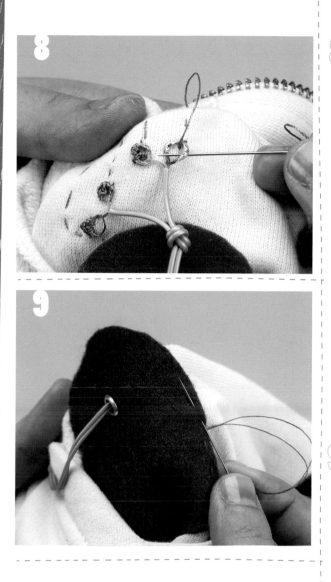

SEW LOOPS

Thread one tail of conductive thread near the pocket into a needle. Push the needle through to the inside of the pocket. Place the plug wire loops so that the 2 loops of 1 wire are attached to the thread sewn to the right side of the hood and so that the loops of the other wire are attached to the thread sewn to the left side of the hood. Sew 1 loop from the plug wire to the inside of the pocket by inserting the needle into the fabric, exiting through the loop, and wrapping around the loop without going into the fabric. Repeat 3 times for each loop. Go back through the fabric, knot the thread, and cut the excess. Go to the opposite end of the same thread and sew the thread in the same way around the earphone loop of the same color.

Repeat the process for each end of the other threads, making sure that each plug wire loop is connected by the conductive thread to the earphone wire loop of the same color.

COVER LOOPS

Use a needle and sewing thread to topstitch the heart inside the pocket. Topstitch 1 large felt flower to the inside of the hood to cover the left earphone, and topstitch 1 large flower on the outside of the hood to help keep the left earphone in place. Repeat for the right earphone. Topstitch the small flower to embellish the hoodie, adding more small flowers if desired.

WASH WITH CARE

If your hoodie needs a cleaning, first cover the speaker components (anything under the felt pieces) in plastic bags with rubber bands. Then hand-wash the rest of the hoodie and let it drip dry.

ALTERNATIVE HEADPHONE HOODIE DESIGN

If hearts and flowers aren't your thing, try making this project with the cloud and square patterns on page 122.

LIGHTNING BUG COSTUME

TECHNIQUES

Creating a seam allowance, page 16

Backstitching, page 16

Pinning and cutting patterns, page 18

Pressing seam allowances, page 18

Pinning fabric pieces, page 19

MATERIALS

green tulle (refer to step 1 on page 100 for length)

white woven fabric (refer to step 1 on page 100 for length)

EL wire, the thinnest type available

driver for EL wire

batteries for driver

green or white satin ribbon, 2" (5cm) wide (refer to step 6 on page 102 for length)

white thread

green thread

safety pin

scissors

pins

measuring tape

sewing machine

pen and notepaper

iron

Shortly after I was on *Project Runway*, I was invited to Heidi Klum's Halloween party. I wanted to wear something neat that stood out, so I created a costume that glowed: a lightning bug costume. Like that costume, this adaptation has a tulle skirt with EL wire sewed into the hem to make it light up. Add a tank top, a pair of wings, and maybe even some antennae, and you'll be the hit of your next Halloween party!

MEASURE AND CUT SKIRT FABRIC

Use a measuring tape to measure your high waist, which is level or a little above your belly button (see the diagram below). Write down this measurement for step 7. Multiply the high-waist measurement by 3. This is the length of the white woven fabric and green tulle you need to purchase. For example, if your high waist measurement is 30" (76cm), then you need 90" (2.3m) of each fabric.

Measure from your high waist to your knee. Multiply this by $3/5$. For the height of the white woven fabric, add 1" (3cm) to this answer. For the height of the green tulle, add $2\frac{1}{4}$" (6cm) to this answer. For example, if the length from your high waist to your knee is 25" (64cm), the number is 15" = 25" x $3/5$ (38cm = 64cm x $3/5$), so the height of the white woven fabric is 16" = 15" + 1" (41cm = 38cm + 3cm) and the height of the green tulle is $17\frac{1}{4}$" = 15" + $2\frac{1}{4}$" (44cm = 38cm + 6cm). Cut the white woven fabric and the green tulle to these measurements. If your fabric isn't long enough, you can cut several pieces that are the correct height and sew them together.

STEADY HANDS

When cutting fabric, hold the scissors flush to the table in one hand and use the other hand to hold down the fabric.

BUYING EL WIRE

When purchasing EL wire, be sure to buy a driver, a little box with special electronics that turn the EL wire on and off. A driver usually has a compartment for batteries, but sometimes the batteries are external.

To find your high-waist measurement, wrap a tape measure around your waist near your belly button. Use this measurement in step 1.

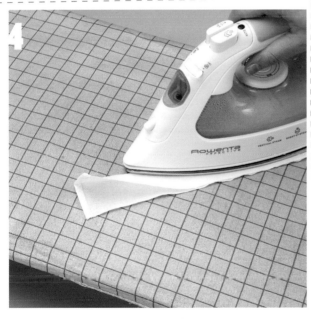

CREATE ROLLED HEM

Fold the long edge of the white woven fabric up
¼" (6mm) and then fold it up the same amount
again. This prevents the hem from fraying. As you
sew the hem, you can crease the fabric with your
fingernail to help hold it in place, or you can pin it
down for more security. Use white thread, a sewing machine, and a straight stitch to sew the hem
at the edge of the fold.

SEW HEM IN TULLE

Fold the long edge of the green tulle up ¾" (2cm).
Use green thread to straight stitch the hem with
a ½" (1cm) fold on one side and a ¼" (6mm) raw
edge on the other.

CREATE AND PRESS WAISTBAND

Cut a piece of woven fabric that is 5" (13cm)
wide and the length of the fabric from step 1 (the
example is 90" [2.3m]). Finish the ends of the
waistband with a ¼" (6mm) rolled hem, as in step
2. Fold the waistband in half lengthwise and press
it with an iron. The result is a waistband that's
2½" (6cm) high.

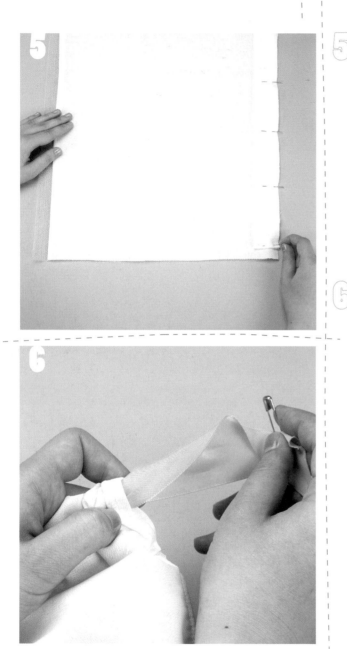

5 ATTACH WAISTBAND

Lay the tulle piece so the hemmed edge is facing down. Lay the woven fabric piece so the hemmed edge is facing down onto the tulle. Align the short ends of the two pieces. The hemmed edge of the tulle should extend 1" (3cm) past the hemmed edge of the woven fabric. Lay 1 short end of the waistband ½" (1cm) in from the edge of the fabric and the tulle, aligning the waistband's long edge with the raw long edges of the fabric and the tulle. Pin the waistband, tulle and woven fabric together. Using a sewing machine and a ½" (1cm) seam allowance, sew these 3 pieces together.

6 THREAD RIBBON

Cut a piece of ribbon that's a little longer than the fabric's length measurement from step 1. For that example, the measurement is 90" (2.3m), so the ribbon should be about 100" (2.5m). Press the waistband up with the seam allowance facing down toward the skirt's hemmed edges. Attach a safety pin to 1 end of the ribbon. Push the safety pin and ribbon into 1 opening of the waistband and feed the safety pin and the ribbon through the waistband, bunching the fabric as you go. Continue pushing the safety pin and bunching the fabric until you've threaded the ribbon through the entire waistband, exiting out the other end of the waistband. An equal amount of ribbon should extend out of each side.

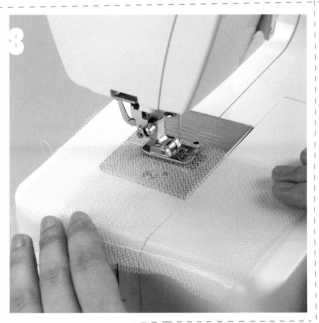

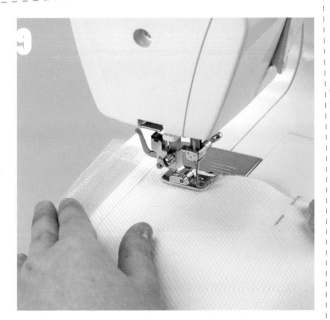

TACK RIBBON TO WAISTBAND

Multiply the high-waist measurement from step 1 by 1¼; for that example, 30" x 1¼ = 37½" (76cm x 1¼ = 95cm). On the waistband, measure this distance (e.g., 37½" [95cm]) from each end across the waistband and mark each of these 2 points with a pin. Using white thread and a sewing machine, straight stitch a 2½" (6cm) vertical line where each pin is; stitch only through the waistband to secure the ribbon.

CREATE DRIVER POCKET

Measure the height and width of the driver and battery pack. Double the height and add ½" (1cm); add 2" (5cm) to the width. Cut a piece of tulle to this size. Fold the tulle nearly in half; leave ½" (1cm) at the top. Using green thread, a sewing machine and a ½" (1cm) seam allowance, straight stitch the 2 long sides. Do not turn this pocket inside out.

SEW BACK OF SKIRT

Fold the skirt in half widthwise, with the white fabric on the inside and the sides of the skirt aligned. Using a sewing machine, straight stitch a ½" (1cm) seam allowance and sew the skirt sides together from the hemmed edges to the bottom of the waistband. This seam will be at the back of the skirt.

10 FINISH BACK SEAM

Press open the seam. Stitch down each side of the seam allowance, leaving at least ¼" (6mm) between the back seam and each new line of stitching.

11 ATTACH DRIVER POCKET

With the tulle side of the skirt up, fold down the waistband, exposing the seam allowance you left in step 5. Lay the ½" (1cm) top edge of the pocket from step 8 against the tulle, aligning it with the top edge of the waistband seam allowance and about 4" (10cm) away from the back seam you sewed in step 9. Using a sewing machine, straight stitch the pocket to the seam allowance.

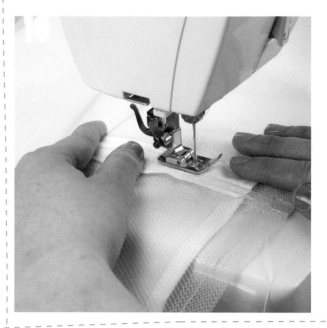

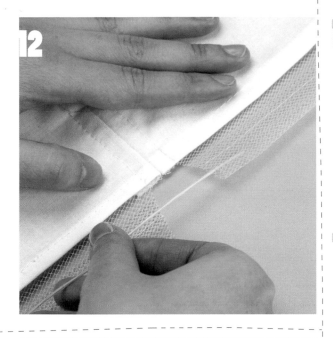

12 ADD EL WIRE

At the back seam in step 9 (the center stitch-line of the 3 stitchlines), cut the tulle from the hem to the edge of the white fabric. Push the plain end of the EL wire through the tulle hem so that the EL wire runs all the way around the skirt. You can bend the end of the EL wire into a U shape so it won't snag on the tulle as you push it through. If you have extra EL wire, thread it up through one of the channels you created next to the back seam in step 10.

13 CONNECT EL WIRE TO DRIVER

Place the driver in the pocket. Connect the driver to the EL wire. To wear the skirt, pull the ribbon around your waist, gathering the waistband as you go, and tie the ribbon in a bow. The driver will be on the inside of the skirt. If any of the wires hang out from beneath the hem of the skirt, secure them in place with safety pins. Or hand sew them to the tulle with matching thread.

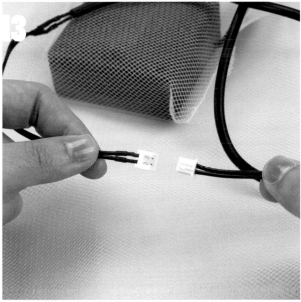

CREATE A LIGHT-UP HEADBAND

Want to add some super cute antennae to your costume? Prepare two plastic containers like you did in step 4 of the *Blooming Buttons* project on page 82. Solder an LED to a BS7 battery holder, and glue the battery holder to the lid of the container using a hot glue gun. Repeat for the second container. Glue the lids of the containers to a wide headband. Remove the domed part of each container to insert the battery and light up the LED.

LIKE A LIGHTNING BUG

By tying the bow in the back, and gathering the tulle near the bow, you'll create a nice poof of fabric. When you connect the EL wire, your rear will light up just like a lightning bug!

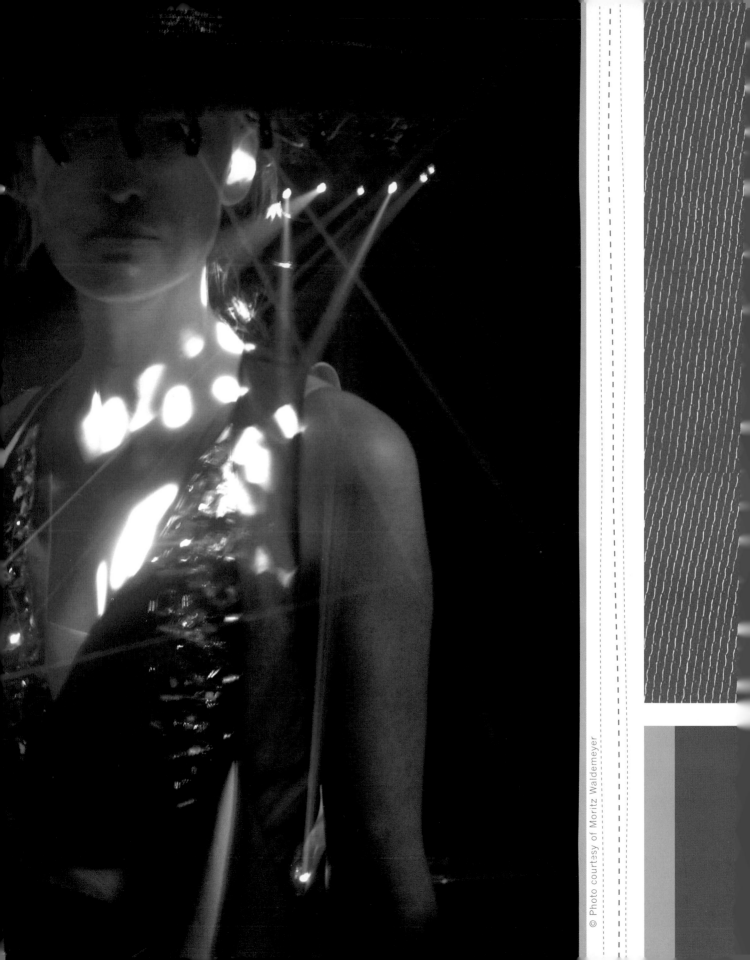

GALLERY

Here is a collection of some of the latest and most fashion-forward technology.
These fashions—made by scientists, researchers, designers and crafters—
have been on stage and walked down the runway. This gallery is filled with
projects that have elements similar to those in the projects in this book.
The OK Go jackets (page 110) and the Video Dress (page 108) use LEDs.
Becky Stern's LilyPad Embroidery (page 112) has an embroidered circuit
like the one in *Shirt Circuit* on page 88. The Accouphene tuxedo (page 111)
has a jacket that creates sounds. Like *Headphone Hoodie* on page 92,
Accouphene uses conductive thread to replace the wires of speakers.
I hope that you will use this gallery as inspiration while you make the
Fashion Geek projects or design some of your own.

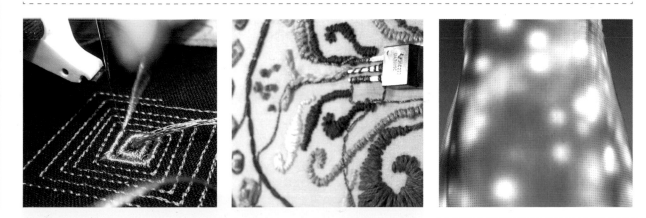

VIDEO DRESS

The Airborne Video Dresses are a collaboration between Hussein Chalayan and Moritz Waldemeyer. The surface of the dress can display video imagery enabled by fifteen thousand individually controllable LEDs embedded beneath the fabric. One dress displays hazy silhouettes of sharks in the sea, while the other shows a time-lapse sequence of a rose blooming then closing. The effect is mesmerizing in its ambiguity: the loose white fabric covering the LEDs blurs and distorts the images so that they seem to pulsate in and out of existence.

LIGHT-UP ZIPPER HOODIE

I created this hoodie with an embroidered LED pattern controlled by the zipper. The zipper acts as a switch, turning different parts of the LED pattern on and off. As the zipper gets zipped closed, circuits close and LEDs turn on. As more of the zipper gets zipped, more of the pattern illuminates.

© Photo by Andre Walker

OK GO JACKETS

During their recent performance, OK Go literally lit up the stage with Moritz Waldemeyer's latest creation of thousands of LEDs stitched onto the band members' jackets. The flickering lights of slot machines in Las Vegas casinos inspired Waldemeyer to create these innovative stage costumes that blend perfectly into OK Go's own synthesis of power pop and tongue-in-cheek wit. When the band takes the stage, the LEDs embedded in their jackets run through a sequence that makes up the letters O K G O, like a slot machine spinning its symbols and spelling the band's name.

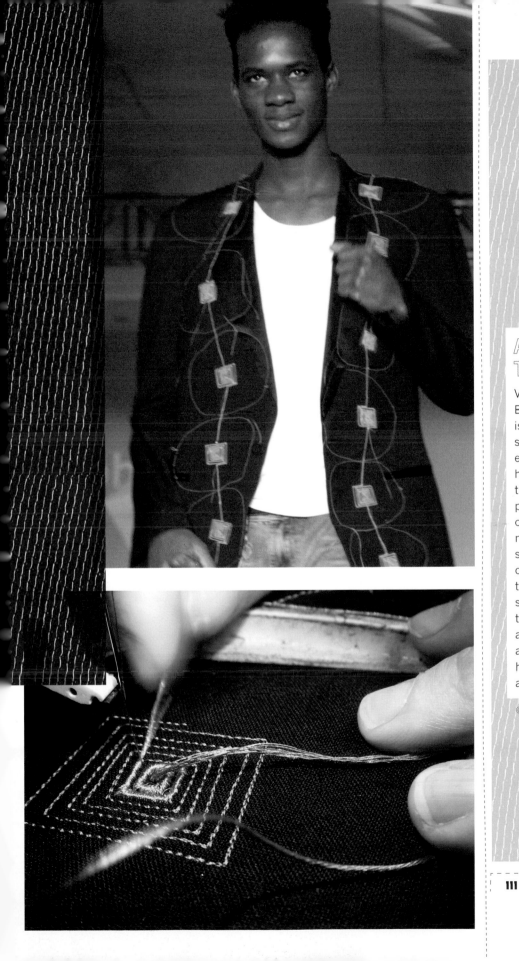

ACCOUPHENE TUXEDO

Vincent Leclerc and Joanna Berzowska's Accouphene tuxedo is decorated with thirteen soft speakers made functional by embroidered decorative coils of highly conductive yarn (similar to the conductive thread used in the projects in this book) on the front of the jacket. The coils are connected to a central circuit, which sends pulses of energy through the coils. Sounds are generated when the sleeves, which each contain a stitched magnet, are moved over the coils. A 3-D sonic environment around the human body can be activated and modulated through hand movement and the twisting and compression of the cloth.

© Photos by James Patten

111

LED BRACELET

This LED bracelet was woven on a traditional bead loom using beads, conductive thread and surface-mount LEDs. Leah Buechley designed the bracelets to be beautiful whether the electricity is on or off. The LEDs form a 5x10 display matrix that can have scrolling text or moving patterns. These LED bracelets can sense motion, and they have Bluetooth for wireless communication to interact with laptops, cell phones and PDAs.

LILYPAD EMBROIDERY

This needlework sampler by Becky Stern incorporates electronic components and conductive thread. It uses Leah Buechley's LilyPad Arduino, a microcontroller board designed specifically to be sewn and to control lights and sounds generated by the onboard software. The circuit senses light levels, which determine the speed and pitch of the lights and sounds generated.

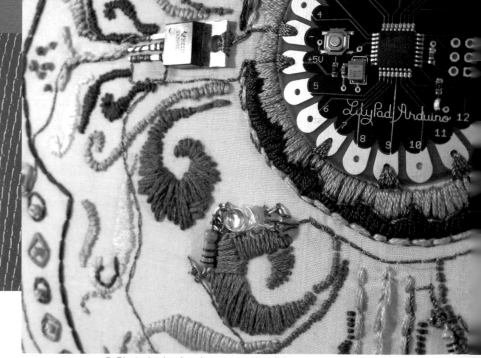

© Photo courtesy of Moritz Waldemeyer

LASER DRESS

Hussein Chalayan collaborated with Moritz Waldemeyer to create the laser dresses in the spring 2008 collection "Readings" unveiled at Paris Fashion Week. Inspired by themes of ancient sun worship and the contemporary phenomenon of celebrity, the laser dresses literally emanate light. The dresses create bold silhouettes from which the laser beams radiate. The dresses are embellished with Swarovski crystals that either deflect the lasers or take in their light, depending on the angle of the laser. Hundreds of lasers were integrated into each piece and attached by custom-designed, servo-driven brass hinges. This allows the lasers to move, transforming the dresses from static objects to living, ephemeral forms that constantly change and interact with the space around them. The result is one of the most dynamic examples of a new fusion where fashion and design meet, each enhancing the other.

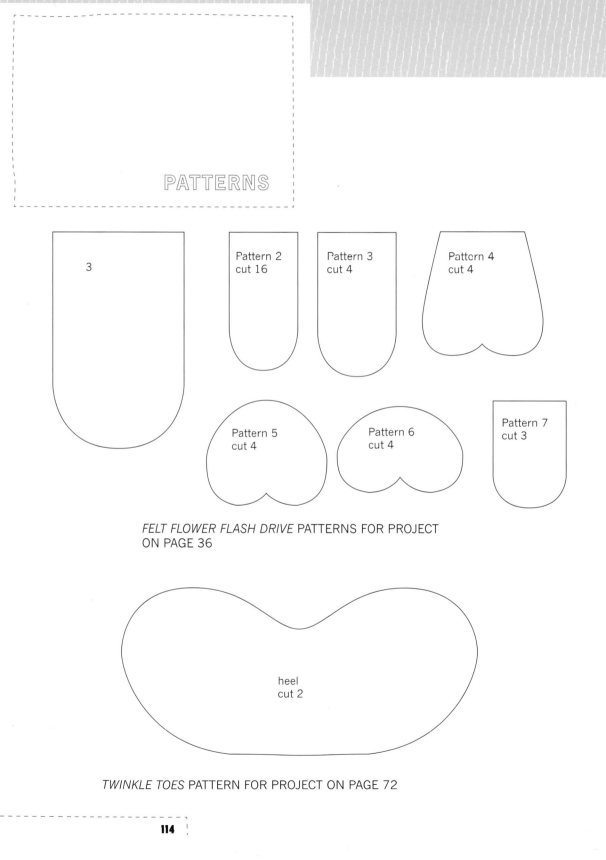

PATTERNS

3

Pattern 2
cut 16

Pattern 3
cut 4

Pattern 4
cut 4

Pattern 5
cut 4

Pattern 6
cut 4

Pattern 7
cut 3

FELT FLOWER FLASH DRIVE PATTERNS FOR PROJECT
ON PAGE 36

heel
cut 2

TWINKLE TOES PATTERN FOR PROJECT ON PAGE 72

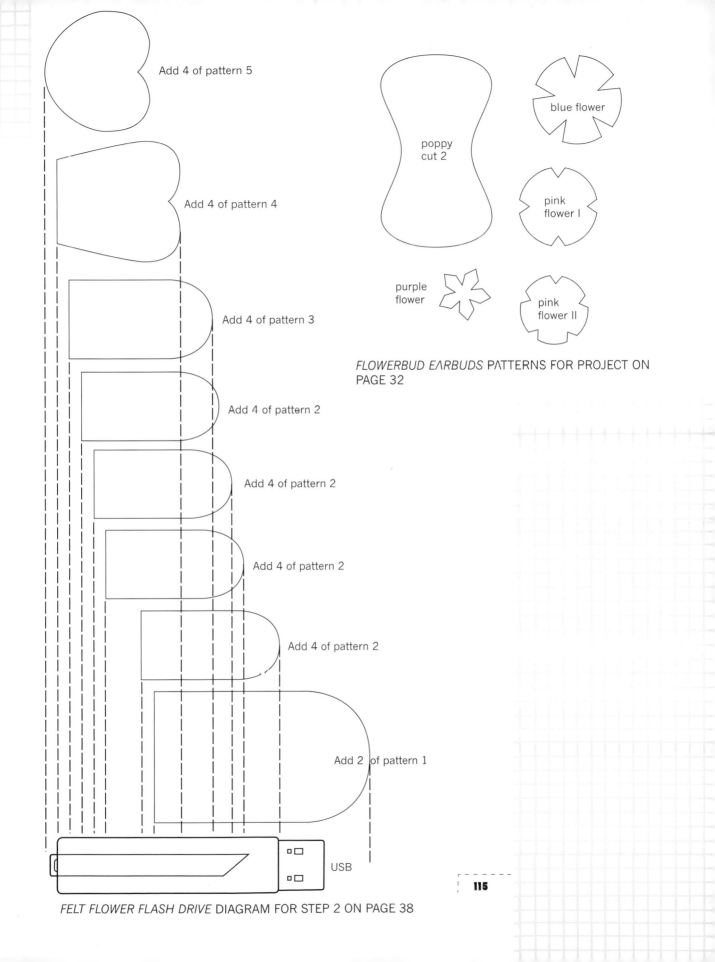

Add 4 of pattern 5

Add 4 of pattern 4

Add 4 of pattern 3

Add 4 of pattern 2

Add 4 of pattern 2

Add 4 of pattern 2

Add 4 of pattern 2

Add 2 of pattern 1

USB

FELT FLOWER FLASH DRIVE DIAGRAM FOR STEP 2 ON PAGE 38

poppy
cut 2

blue flower

pink
flower I

purple
flower

pink
flower II

FLOWERBUD EARBUDS PATTERNS FOR PROJECT ON
PAGE 32

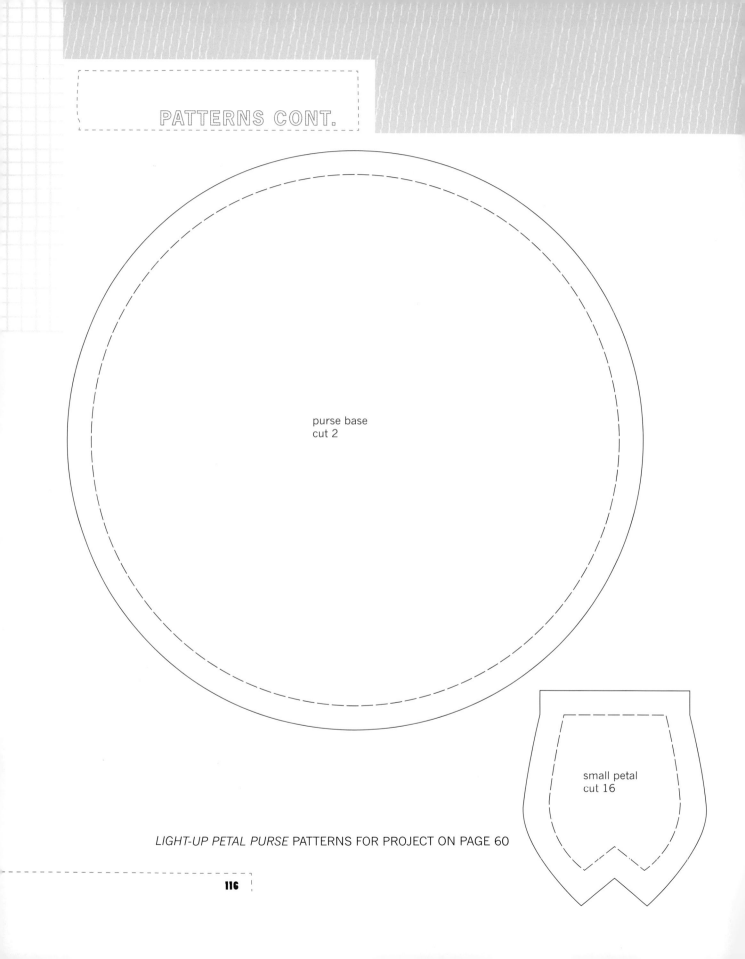

purse base
cut 2

small petal
cut 16

LIGHT-UP PETAL PURSE PATTERNS FOR PROJECT ON PAGE 60

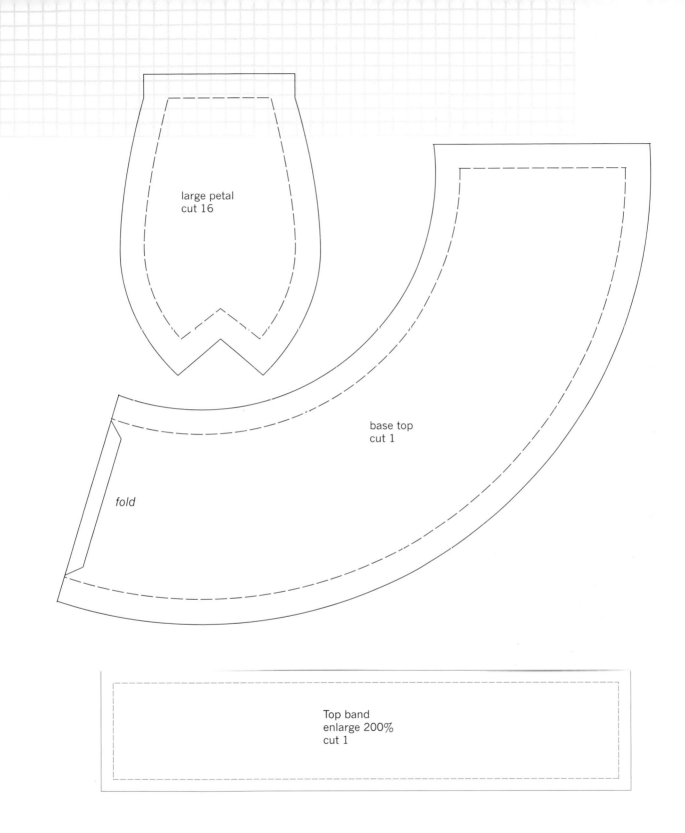

large petal
cut 16

base top
cut 1

fold

Top band
enlarge 200%
cut 1

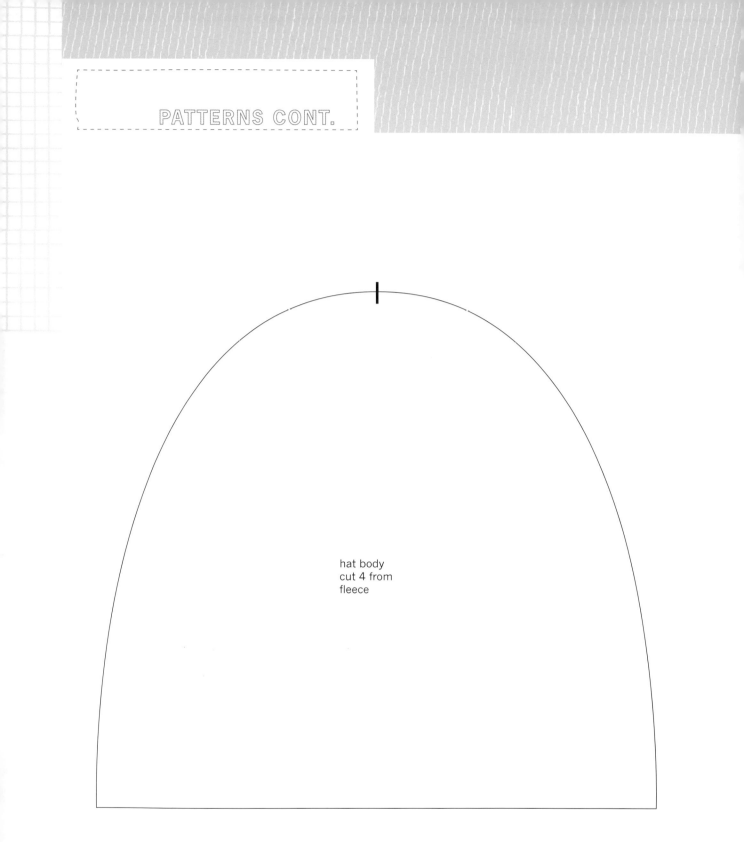

hat body
cut 4 from
fleece

MONSTER MUSIC HAT PATTERNS FOR PROJECT ON PAGE 50

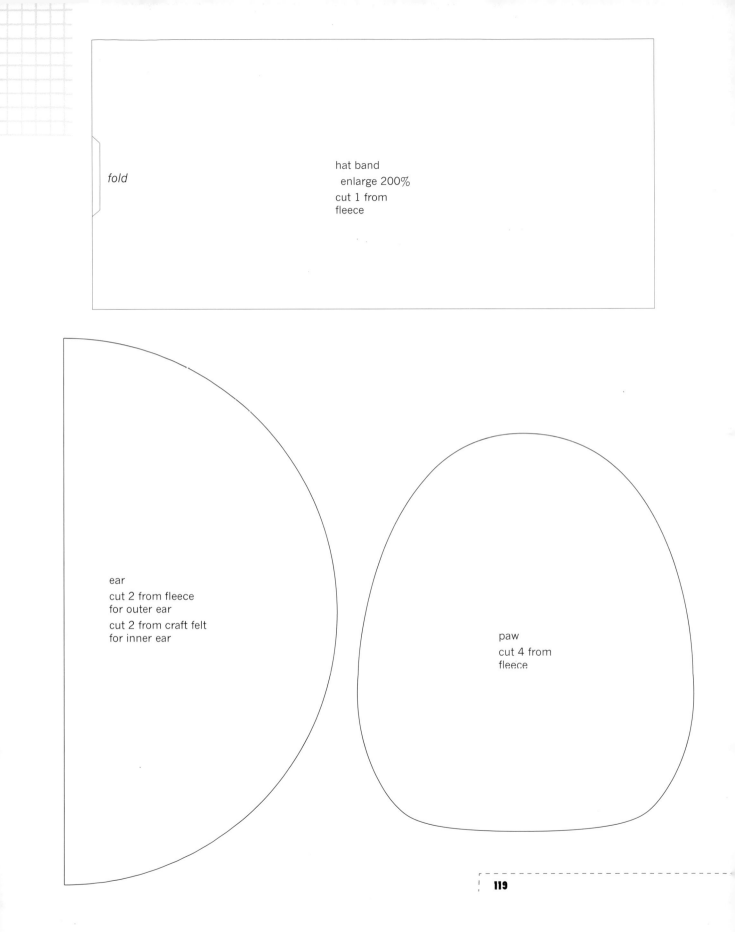

fold

hat band
 enlarge 200%
cut 1 from
fleece

ear
cut 2 from fleece
for outer ear
cut 2 from craft felt
for inner ear

paw
cut 4 from
fleece

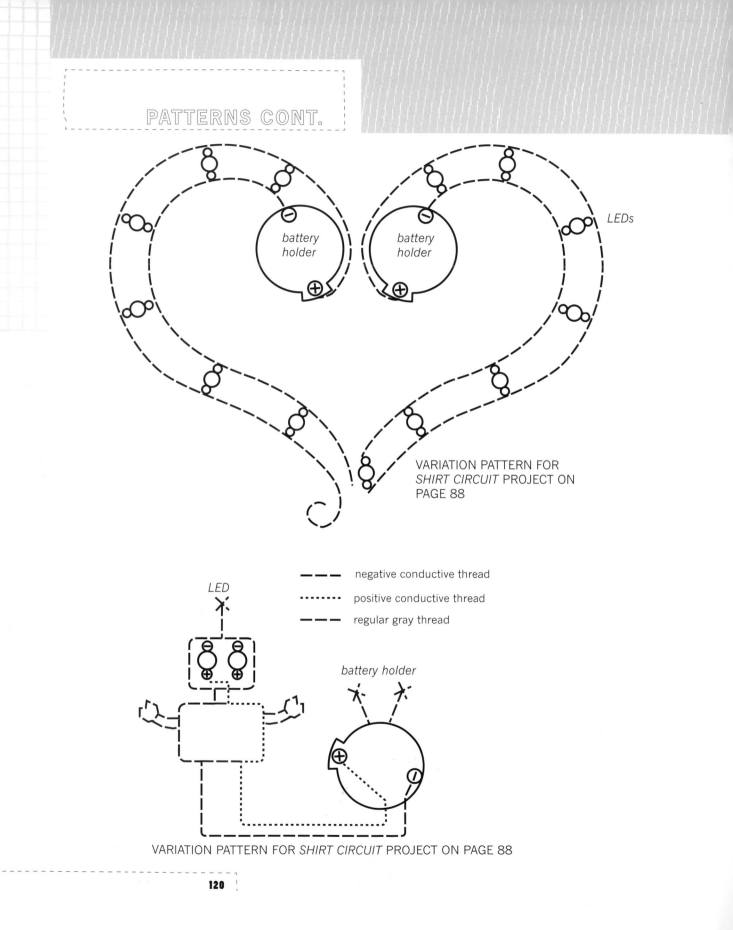

LEDs

battery holder

battery holder

VARIATION PATTERN FOR
SHIRT CIRCUIT PROJECT ON
PAGE 88

LED

— — —   negative conductive thread

· · · · ·   positive conductive thread

– – –   regular gray thread

battery holder

VARIATION PATTERN FOR *SHIRT CIRCUIT* PROJECT ON PAGE 88

LED

battery holder

SHIRT CIRCUIT PATTERN FOR
PROJECT ON PAGE 88
enlarge 125%

VARIATION PATTERN FOR
SHIRT CIRCUIT PROJECT
ON PAGE 88

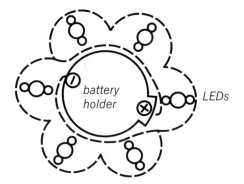

battery holder

LEDs

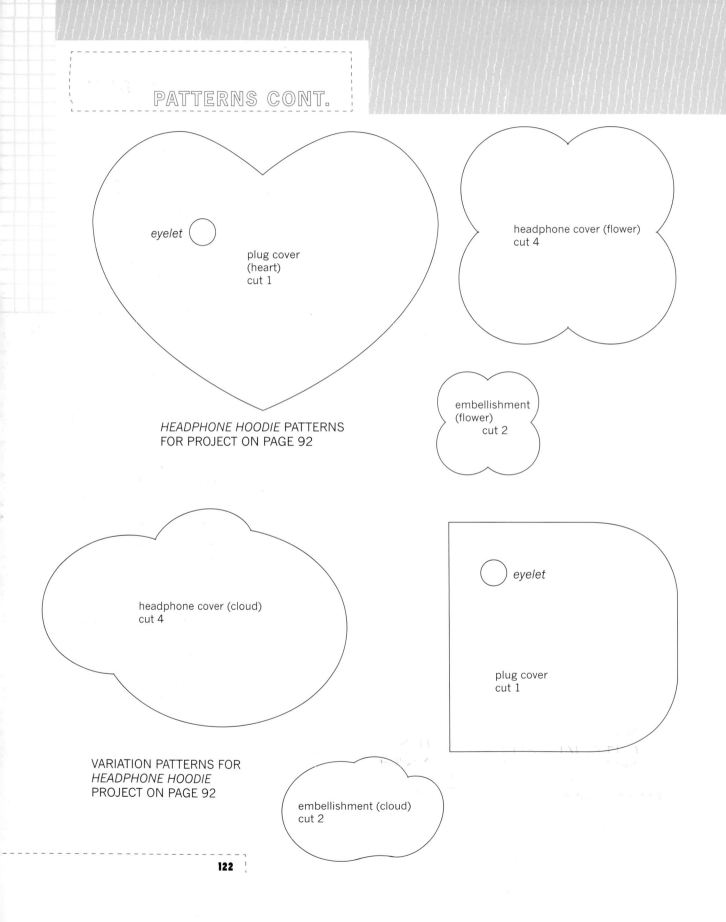

eyelet

plug cover
(heart)
cut 1

headphone cover (flower)
cut 4

HEADPHONE HOODIE PATTERNS
FOR PROJECT ON PAGE 92

embellishment
(flower)
cut 2

headphone cover (cloud)
cut 4

eyelet

plug cover
cut 1

VARIATION PATTERNS FOR
HEADPHONE HOODIE
PROJECT ON PAGE 92

embellishment (cloud)
cut 2

ALLIGATOR CLIP JUMPER WIRES: Two spring-loaded clips connected by a wire in between. Alligator clips are used to make temporary electronic connections and will be handy to help you test a circuit.

CIRCUIT: The closed path formed by connecting electronic components together so that electric current can flow through them.

CONDUCTIVE THREAD: Thread that allows electricity to flow through it, like wire. Conductive thread usually has metal bonded with it on the molecular level.

CONTACT: The metal part of an electronic component that is connected to a circuit.

DRIVER (FOR EL WIRE): A driver is a special device used to make EL wire glow. In order for EL wire to glow, it must have a high voltage connected to it. The circuit inside of the driver does exactly this. All you need to do is plug the EL wire into the driver, and the driver will make the EL wire glow.

EL WIRE: Short for *electroluminescent wire*, this wire is coated with a thin layer of phosphor and glows with electric current.

ELECTRICAL TAPE: Tape used to insulate wires and other conductive materials.

EYE PIN: A thin metal piece with a loop on the end. It is used for making jewelry.

GROMMETS: Metal rings used to reinforce holes.

HELPING HANDS: Tool used in electronics to help hold parts while they are being soldered.

JEWELRY PLIERS: A type of pliers with an extremely long and narrow gripping nose typically used for working with jewelry, but used for electronics projects in this book.

LEAD: The long metal contact of an electronic component.

LED (pronounced el-ee-dee): Short for light-emitting diode. An electronic component that lights up. Since LEDs are diodes, electricity can only flow through them in one direction. The positive side of the circuit must be connected to the long lead of an LED, and the negative side of the circuit must be connected to the short lead.

NEEDLE-NOSE PLIERS: A type of pliers that have a long gripping nose.

PHOTORESISTOR: A light-sensitive resistor whose resistance decreases when there is more light. A photoresistor allows more electric current to pass through when there is more light and less electric current to pass through when there is less light.

PLIERS: A tool used to help grip and hold small objects.

PONY BEADS: A popular style of craft bead.

RARE EARTH MAGNET: A very strong magnet made from alloys of rare earth elements.

RAW EDGE: An unfinished edge of a piece of fabric.

REED SWITCH: A switch that turns on and off when near a magnetic field.

RESISTOR: An electronic component that helps control the amount of electric current in a circuit by creating a voltage drop.

ROTARY TOOL: A handheld rotating power tool with attachments that can be used for cutting, drilling, sanding and polishing. A popular brand of rotary tool is Dremel.

RUNNING STITCH: The most basic stitch, made by passing a needle into and out of fabric. Also called a *straight stitch*.

SEAM ALLOWANCE: The space between the edge of a piece of fabric and the stitch line.

SOLDER/SOLDERING: A metal alloy with a low melting point. It is used for connecting electronics.

SOLDERING IRON: A tool used to melt solder so that it can be used to connect electronics (like a glue gun does for glue).

STRAIGHT STITCH: See *running stitch*.

STRIPPING WIRE: Removing the outer protective coating on a wire to create an electrical connection with the wire inside.

TINNING: Covering a contact (such as a lead or wire) with a thin layer of solder before soldering the contacts together to help create a better electrical connection.

TRACING PAPER: Translucent paper of light quality usually used by artists for tracing drawings.

WIRE: A long metal strand used to carry electricity.

WIRE CUTTER: A tool used to cut wire. It is sometimes built into pliers.

ZIGZAG STITCH: A type of stitch forming a zigzag pattern, which resembles a lightning bolt. Each stitch alternates direction.

RESOURCES

The items you'll need to create the projects in this book are available from a variety of sources. Your local electronics store is likely to carry some of the items needed. These online sources will be helpful as well.

ELECTRONIC PARTS:

The following sites offer all electronic items used in this book, including LEDs, photoresistors, reed switches, BS7 battery holders, CR2023 batteries, and soldering tools.

Digi-Key
www.digikey.com

Jameco Electronics
www.jameco.com

Mouser Electronics
www.mouser.com

EL WIRE AND DRIVERS:

Cool Neon
www.coolneon.com
My source for the EL wire and drivers used in this book. Note that they call EL wire "Cool Neon wire."

CooLight
www.coolight.com

Live Wire
www.elbestbuy.com

DIGITAL PHOTO KEY CHAIN:

These are becoming increasingly available at camera stores, electronic stores and even discount department stores. The various online sources include:

TAO
www.taoelectronics.com
My source for the digital keychain used in this book.

CONDUCTIVE THREAD:

Lamé Lifesaver
members.shaw.ca/ubik/thread/order.html
This thread is my favorite to use.

SparkFun Electronics
www.sparkfun.com
Buy the two-ply thread, not the four-ply thread, when shopping at this site.

Adafruit.com ~ Youtube channel - ~~unreleased~~ ~~Rachel [illegible]~~

Beginner LED sewing Kit #1285 $14.95

thread, 2 batt. holders, 2 batteries, 4 LED's, 4 sugds, needles

ELECTRICAL SOLDER:

Available at most hardware stores and electronics stores.

RARE EARTH MAGNETS:

K&J Magnetics, Inc.
www.kjmagnetics.com
I used R313 magnets for the *Blooming Buttons* project on page 82.

REFERENCE BOOKS:

Getting Started in Electronics, by Forrest M. Mims III. Published by Master Publishing, Inc.

If you have enjoyed working with electronics and would like to learn more, read this book. It has a very in-depth look at all the electronics basics and will help you learn about building circuits from different components like LEDs, resistors, capacitors, diodes, inductors, transistors, ICs, switches.

Complete Guide to Sewing by the Editors of Readers' Digest. Published by Reader's Digest.

If you would like to learn more about sewing, here is the book I always refer to. It very easy to understand instructions for every sewing technique imaginable.

CONTRIBUTORS:

Leah Buechley

MIT Media Lab

www.media.mit.edu/~leah

Vincent Leclerc and Joanna Berzowska
www.uttermatter.com
www.xslabs.net

Accouphene tuxedo © 2006 XS Labs

LilyPad Arduino

www.arduino.cc/en/Main/ArduinoBoardLilyPad

Sternlab
www.sternlab.org
Visit this site for more information, a demonstration video, and a tutorial on how to add electronics to embroidery.

Moritz Waldemeyer
www.waldemeyer.com

Andre Walker
www.andrewalkerweddings.com

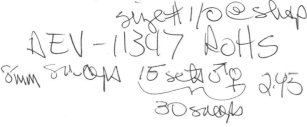

size #1/0 @ shop
DEV-11347 RoHS
8mm snaps 15 sets of 2.95
30 snaps

INDEX

Mr. Funky's Super Crochet Wonderful is filled with 25 supercute crochet patterns for adorable Japanese-style stuffed animals and accessories. You'll find candy-color elephants, panda bears, kitty cats, hamsters and even a snake, plus fashionable hats, armwarmers and purses for girls of all ages. Each pattern features written out instructions as well as traditional amigurumi, or Japanese crochet, diagrams.

ISBN 10: 1-58180-966-2
ISBN 13: 978-1-58180-966-4
paperback | 112 pages | Z0697

Check out **AlterNation**, the DIY fashion Bible, that shows you how to personalize your wardrobe with a wide range of no-sew and low-sew techniques. This book has lots of stuff to make, like tie skirts, scrap scarves, plus oh so much more. Just follow the step-by-step instructions, and you'll soon be a pro at making your own clothing and accessories.

ISBN-10: 1-58180-978-6
ISBN-13: 978-1-58180-978-7
paperback | 144 pages | Z0713

Plush You This showcase of 100 plush toys, many with patterns and instructions, will inspire you to join in on the toy phenomenon. The simple projects in this book provide instant gratification for beginners and new ideas and inspiration for experienced toymakers. Stuffed space creatures and lovable monsters, along with the occasional cut of beef and other squeezable subjects make this an irresistible book that you just want to hug.

ISBN-10: 1-58180-996-4
ISBN-13: 978-1-58180-996-1
paperback with flaps | 144 pages | Z0951

In **Print Liberation**, graphic artists and screen printers Nick Paparone and Jamie Dillon will give you the know-how you need to start screen printing at home today. You can even use the screen-print-ready images created by the authors in your own screen prints. With screen printing basics and step-by-step instructions for a variety of techniques, this is the definitive guide for both novice and experienced artists.

ISBN-10: 1-60061-072-2
ISBN-13: 978-1-60061-072-1
paperback | 144 pages | Z1819

These books and other fine North Light titles are available at your local craft retailer, bookstore or online supplier, or visit us at www.mycraftivity.com.